"It's not often we come across those in our industry of helping youth & families through the difficult issues of life, who not only "get it", but can articulate it in a way to influence others to "get it". In, *God, Help Me Tie My Shoes*, Tony Goulet has written a powerful and masterful narrative that offers insight, wisdom and truth. This important message will no doubt bring help, healing, and transformation to youth & parents in all generations. Tony's voice is needed in the work of violence prevention amongst our youth and neighborhoods across America. He speaks to the *root solution* of turning the hearts of parents and children towards one another in a learned lifestyle of love, forgiveness and reconciliation. This book will teach you how. It is a must read for youth as well as parents, teachers, and social workers laboring to provide youth the self respect to choose the right path to their true potential."

~ Richard Ramos, Founder of "Parents On a Mission"

"This beautiful creation by Anthony Goulet is as powerful as it is touching. It engages the reader at a spirit level as you walk in the untied shoes of a troubled teen as he experiences pain, loss, anger, and ultimately healing, personal strength and forgiveness. This is a book every adult and youth in our communities should read! Anthony Goulet shares a story, both tender and real, that empower us with a message to love our kids in the deepest way – to simply be there for them. We don't need to have all the answers, but just be there – not later, not when it's convenient, but now. Later may be too late. Way to go Anthony – you've shared a priceless insight into the often secret lives of our youth so we can better support and encourage them to be strong and successful in this world!"

~ D.J. Eagle Bear Vanas, Author of The Tiny Warrior: A Path to Personal Discovery & Achievement

Dedication

This book is first and foremost dedicated to The Author of all life, The Creator. Thank you for giving humanity new eyes to see You in all that You've created.

To my children, thank you for awakening my heart to all that is real.

To my biological dad, my dad who raised me, and my adopted dad, thank you for your time and love.

To my mother, you are the strongest woman I've ever known, thank you for everything, and I love you.

To my lovely wife, thank you for all your patience and for being a living example of hope.

Acknowledgements

I thank The Creator for the Love, Faith, Hope and Charity that we as humanity have been given to share with one another.

Thank you to Dolores and Mike Salinas. Your love and dedication shines brightly through the blessings we share in this life.

Thank you to my Uncle Clare Sanders for guiding me through every transition in my life. Thank you for your consistency, living your dreams and being a wonderful example of a healthy and healed man.

Thank you to my Uncle Tome Roubideaux. You have enriched every aspect of my life with your love, patience, compassion, and guidance.

Thank you to Susan Forward Ph.D. for allowing me to use her analogy of the FOG – Fear, Obligation, and Guilt within a portion of this book.

Thank you to Mike Vazquez who has always said, "Youth work is Spirit led, if it's not Spirit led, then it's not youth work." Thank you for being a true servant leader.

Thank you to all of my grandparents, brothers, sisters, aunties, uncles, nieces, nephews, and friends. Your love and prayers helped make this book possible.

Thank you to all of the ancestors who endured so much. I thank you for your courage, fortitude, wisdom and charity.

Thank you to the next seven generations for choosing the path that has been placed within each one of your hearts by The Great One.

Foreword

When Anthony asked me to read his manuscript and compose a foreword I was honored. I have known Anthony for close to twenty years and I have witnessed the patience and kindness he has shown to the youth and heard the success stories of many people with whom he has worked.

Although *God, Help Me Tie My Shoes! The Sacred Contract of Fatherhood* and the young person telling his story are fictional the contents of this book are derived from real events and people that we can see and feel inside our own hearts and memories.

Carlos' story is one of those realities that most of us merely accept but few actually dedicate their lives to exact some sort of positive change or influence. Fewer people genuinely care about the wellbeing and growth of the generations through actual work with children. This work should be honored and appreciated because it may be the most important work there is.

As the story begins Carlos is a youth from a troubled home in a troubled place. Carlos, his mother and little brother are some of the nameless images we so often see on TV struggling to just survive the gauntlet of the world and community that surrounds them. So many youth are lost to the cynicism of this world where many people simply resign to the notion that they can't do anything to change the world or the state of affairs. Contrarily if we want our community, country and world to change and improve then we must take action.

We as humans have the power and grace to exact change and influences that may help the generations to grow and overcome obstacles. We all face these obstacles and only we know whether we have *truly* overcome them or not. If we have overcome our own challenges we most likely are able to identify someone in our formative years that had great influence in our lives. Someone we remember and love merely because they stood by us unconditionally and lovingly.

We are responsible to the children we bring into the world and to the children that look to us for guidance and strength; this is the burden and joy of being adults and parents. It is a burden because it requires us to remove our own expectations and judgments from our interactions with the youth and simply listen. In the story there is a point when Carlos realizes that the youth staff actually listens and takes responsibility for their own shortcomings in front of the youth group. What an amazing concept, to set pride aside and admit even though we are adults we too make mistakes.

Reading this book you will be reminded of the many times in your life when you felt lonely, sad, ignored and abandoned. As well as the times you felt loved, cared for and supported. Those extremes of emotions in the delicate stages of development no matter how old you may be, stir up the memories of those whom were the supportive influences and those you remember as negative. Then the reality hits that you, regardless of your age, you may still bear resentment against parents, teachers or whoever made you feel bad or inadequate.

This is where *God, Help Me Tie My Shoes! The Sacred Contract of Fatherhood* begins to teach us that we must forgive those people that had let us down or harmed us. Not for their sake but for our own so we can forgive ourselves and become the adults, parents and friends our children, families and communities need and deserve. The generations reciprocate by doing well and growing into the best people they can on their own terms.

As *God, Help Me Tie My Shoes! The Sacred Contract of Fatherhood* continues you will feel the need to hug your own children and pour your heart out exclaiming, "I'm only human and I love you." That's the point of our existence anyway, is it not?

We were children once but now those times have passed. So we put the pieces of childhood away in a suitcase, place it in the closet, turn off the lights and close the door only returning when we feel nostalgic or are reminded of joyful or hurtful memories. At times we delve into this suitcase of memories or unresolved issues and completely miss the point of this suitcase we carry - which is to forgive ourselves. For some strange reason, we humans love our misery even if we declare our wishes to be rid of it.

Carlos begins to grow exponentially but after a heartbreaking event he leaves all that has been positive in his life to return to his misery but it doesn't last long because of the wonderful support he has with the youth counselors. The youth counselors teach him how to utilize his perceived mistake as a teaching tool, so he picks himself up and continues on, ultimately facing that which has been his greatest hope and fear.

Whether you're a teenager, adult, elder, parent, professional or student, this book will plant the seeds of change in the hearts and minds of all those who can face themselves long enough to read it all the way through.

Joseph D. Brave-Heart

Dad, Introduce Me to Myself

My name is Carlos. I first went to the after-school prevention program when I was twelve years old and in the seventh grade. Please understand my life story is not about religion. It's about what is supposed to come from whatever religion and culture a person is from, relationships - *healthy relationships*. It's also about how anyone can take any poison, imposed or introduced, and let it be transformed into a healing medicine. The poisons of disappointment, pain, and abandonment were in and all around me. With the guidance of some extraordinary people those poisons were transformed into healing medicines. Remember that if *anything* can happen to someone, it can happen to anyone, this includes miracles too.

My mom thought I needed extra help and more positive influences. She was worried about my behavior. She thought I wasn't doing well in school and hanging around the *wrong crowd* because my dad was in prison. She was right, that was a big part of it. She felt like she needed extra help raising me. She was working two jobs and didn't want me home alone while my little brother was in childcare.

A couple of days before my mom took me to the after-school prevention program I was watching a show on TV. I saw a man talking about growing up in Alaska. He was sharing how he had to watch out for coyotes on his way to school. As I watched that program I remember thinking *on my way to school I have to walk by drug dealers, gangs, and the average jacked up dude that wants to gank you just because. I wish all I had to watch for was coyotes.*

Many days it seemed like some adults in the community would ask me why my grades were low or why I was hanging around *certain* people. Usually when I would try to answer I was interrupted. There was a time I thought those adults really wanted to know about me. After enough interruptions I got used to shrugging my shoulders and saying, "I don't know." One of the reasons I learned to say "I don't know" so much to adults is because they talked *at* me, not *with* me. I learned many adults already had what was supposed to be the *right answer* in their minds, so I learned to say what they wanted to hear or simply say "I don't know."

Regardless of profession, age, or gender there were many different types of adults that influenced us youth. Their influence or lack thereof had everything to do with how they saw themselves. Out of the many different types of influencing perspectives adults offered, three were the most dominant. The one that youth embraced was not the one we heard the most, but the one we *listened* to the most. Directly or indirectly, consciously or subconsciously, spoken or unspoken, adults continuously communicated we were a *problem,* a *victim* or a *gift.*

The adults who saw youth as the *problem* gave us those little *scared straight* talks. They would tell us that if we didn't straighten out we would end up in an early grave or prison. Expectations are powerful and very contagious. Isn't expectation just another way of saying hope? Some of us began to accept the expectations many adults shared with us. I didn't see myself living to be eighteen years old. I didn't want to die. I just began thinking about myself and my future the same way others had spoken it over me and my friends for so long.

The adults that viewed us as *victims* talked to us about being *realistic*. The message from those adults wasn't expectations of imminent failure, death, or imprisonment. The message was *mediocrity*. Those adults attempted to convince us of limited options in life due to who we were, where we lived, and our experiences. They wanted us to be okay with *their* interpretations of our destinies.

Then there were the adults that saw us as a *gift*, an answer to their prayers, a miracle. Those were adults who lived in a manner that reignited the hidden dreams of everyone they encountered. It didn't matter what our behavior was like. They did the opposite of what many people, schools and institutions did to us – they didn't give up. We didn't have to *earn* their respect and love, they gave those gifts unconditionally. They had the ability to show us we *always* had the ability. The gifts they shared helped us dig underneath the pile of brokenness and pain to find the hidden treasures of hope and healing. There are many

in this world as well as in our community. The first ones I
encountered outside of my mom had the title of *youth workers* at
an after-school program. Never did I seek them, to the contrary I
resisted going to where they were. The place I fought going to
was the very place that offered everything I needed at that time.
That was the first of several battles I'm grateful to have lost.

On my first day of the after-school program the ride to
the agency was the worst part. I told my mom for a week that I
didn't want to go to that program. During the drive there I told
her again, "I don't want to go to this stupid program. Why are
you making me go?"

"Until I see some *big* changes in your attitude, friends
and grades you're going to this program. You don't even talk
with me anymore. Carlos, why don't you just talk with me or
your teachers? You're grades are bad and I don't like the kids
your hanging around."

My mom kept talking but her voice became distant.
From the car window I watched as we passed by broken

windows, abandoned-burnt down buildings, and people sitting outside of the liquor stores drinking.

I thought *my grades are the problem here? Maybe there's a reason my grades aren't good. Right now I feel like some of these buildings in our neighborhood, broken and abandoned. I'm just supposed to focus on my grades? I know there are good teachers who care at my school, but why should I talk to them? What are they going to do about my problems? Besides, they're adults and so many adults in the community have already told me I'll be dead or in prison by the time I'm eighteen years old. Maybe I should write my dad again like I have for the past five years every week, even though I haven't gotten one letter back from him. The only people in my life who actually listen to me are the ones some people say I shouldn't be around because they're bad. Funny thing is those bad friends of mine know exactly why my grades are low and why I act up in class sometimes. They might not have any answers for me, most of them are in the same situation I am, but at least they listen.*

There are those who assume youth don't feel or think on a level that some adults consider *deep*. Youth think deeply about most things. Youth's minds haven't been cluttered to the extent many adult minds have, leaving more room for the thoughts of the heart to travel into the mind. The flow of thoughts from the heart to the mind is how the Sacred speaks in and through all of us.

The connection between our hearts and minds is what parents are supposed to cultivate and protect from being broken. Unfortunately that's the first thing in a family to break; leaving behind a long trail of pieces for someone else to pick up...or not. In my community most of our feet were bleeding at a very young age from stepping on the sharp broken pieces of hearts, dreams, and relationships. Some attempted to clean up those pieces. Others tried to put them back together again. Many ignored the pieces which caused them to seek various ways to rid themselves of the pain we walked on and with every day.

I didn't think any adults understood until I went into the after-school prevention program.

Even though I saw other kids I knew from the neighborhood when my mom and I walked into the agency I was nervous. I already had thoughts that something was wrong with me, but I didn't want to hear it from anyone else.

When my mom and I walked into the agency we were greeted by two of the guys that worked there. The first thing I noticed was they didn't tell me to call them *mister* or *sir*. They introduced themselves by their first names. They called themselves youth workers.

During the initial interaction my mom got a little frustrated and asked, "Why are you going to let my son call you by your first names?"

One of the youth workers Rolando smiled really big. "Our titles are not nearly as important as our testimonies; we're not *better* than the youth we serve, we *are* the youth we serve."

I liked how he answered my mom's question. Who doesn't like feeling respected?

Rolando liked to be called Rolo. He was twenty-two years old, athletic, and funny. He was from the neighborhood. I had seen him around and knew who his family was. There was another guy named Dennis. I had seen him give presentations at our school about youth and gang violence. He was a big dude, about thirty something years old. He had a lot of street cred with everyone. He'd been into some bad stuff back in the day, but turned his life around. His *soul*-mission was to offer youth what was not offered to him when he was a teenager.

Dennis and Rolo took my mom and me on a tour of the agency. One of the first things they showed us was music lab. Some kids were recording music and making sweet beats. It was a studio. There was an area where they made t-shirts. Some kids were even putting their own artwork on the silk screen to go on the t-shirts. There were some other kids playing foosball. There was a ping pong table, and an area for basketball. There were kids chillin on a couch talking and watching a movie. Other kids were in the middle sitting in a circle talking. Some were actually doing their homework. The walls were covered in graffiti and I asked Dennis, "Who did the graffiti on the walls?"

"The youth," he said proudly.

It was dope graffiti and I loved to draw. It must have been written all over my face because Dennis told me, "Don't worry, you'll get your chance to have a wall if you stick around."

I knew a lot of the kids in that place and it was packed. I was thinking to myself, *I didn't know these programs had all this.*

During the tour Dennis and Rolo introduced my mom and I to a counselor named Cody. Cody was in his late thirties. He seemed cool enough. I remembered him from around the neighborhood. A few weeks before my first day at the after-school program he rolled up to a group of us that were postin up at the park. He handed out his card telling my friends and me that if we wanted a safe and fun place to hang out we should call the agency and have our parents get us involved. We told him thanks but after he left we threw his cards on the ground and were clownin him.

When Cody welcomed my mom and me he looked at me and it felt like he looked right through me.

"Carlos, what are you willing to die for?"

I was set back with a question like that, "My mom, my little brother and a few other things."

Cody smiled. "You don't have to tell me what the other things are right now. In a little bit of time if you stick around this program you'll find a lot of things you'll want to live for."

Even at twelve years old some kids didn't see living past seventeen or eighteen years old. It didn't matter if you were out there banging, or staying straight and going to school, it was just a reality. A lot of us talked about what we were *down* for, and what we would *die* for. The second he asked me that question I realized it had been a while since I thought about what I was going to *live* for.

Cody excused himself and went back to whatever he was doing. Dennis and Rolo finished giving my mom and me the tour of the agency.

As we walked towards the conference room to go over the program rules and paperwork I asked Rolo, "Does that counselor Cody always ask people those kinds of questions?"

Rolo paused for a moment, looked at me and said, "One thing you will learn about Cody and all the other staff here is that they're pretty spontaneous. There's always a reason for them asking something. I challenge you to stick around long enough to find out what he meant."

We got back to the conference room where my mom filled out paperwork which gave the staff permission to work with me. She explained to them my dad was in prison and wouldn't be out for a while. She started crying when she explained her greatest fear…losing her son to the streets. Dennis and Rolo listened intently and compassionately to her. They told her about another program in the agency for parents, handed her some brochures and invited a lady to come in. The woman asked my mom if she wanted to go talk about other services specifically for her. My mom said, "Yes," and they left the room.

At that point it was only Rolo, Dennis and I at that big table. The only thing comfortable for me was seeing the graffiti on the wall one of the neighborhood kids made. I was thinking *they put his art up in here, that's what's up.*

Rolo asked me, "Are you here because *you* want to be here or because your mom wants you to be here?"

"My mom is worried about me like she said already. She asked at school if there was some help our family could get and they sent us to you guys."

"Look man," Rolo said, "we're not teachers, and this isn't a school. We're not cops, judges, or probation officers. We're here to help kids that want to be part of a positive family."

I shrugged my shoulders. "I'm cool with that."

Dennis insisted, "This agency is neutral territory. Even though some of the youth who come here are active gang members, we don't allow beads, stacking, flagging, or banging. If you wear a hat it will be worn straight forward, straight back, or not worn at all with no exceptions."

"I got it. I understand the rules and don't have a problem with them."

Dennis and Rolo talked with me about my pants not sagging, being respectful, and if I had any problems or complaints to tell the youth staff so they could handle it. I was comfortable with everything they said and how they said it; even the way they explained rules was different than most adults I'd been around until that point in my life.

After my mom finished talking with the lady about programs for parents she came back into the conference room. My mom asked me if I wanted to go home with her or if I wanted to stay and get dropped off later by the youth staff. I told her I would stay and see her later. Before she left, she hugged me, and gave me a kiss on my forehead. After my mom left, Rolo and Dennis took me back into the youth center with everyone else.

They pulled all of us into a big circle. We were supposed to talk about feelings and stuff like that. That was the first time I sat in a circle with people, it felt weird. I pushed through it thinking, *talk about my feelings, heck no. That isn't gonna happen.*

Rolo asked us to answer a question, "Tell me and Dennis without using any reference to music, radio, television, bank accounts, money, or the opposite sex who you are?"

All of us kids were like, "What?!"

Dennis asked the question a little different, "Without anyone or anything else, all by yourselves who are you?"

One of the kids said, "That's impossible because we're all connected to something."

Dennis jumped up and down in his chair and yelled, "Yes! What else?"

All of us were laughing. He was funny but it was making us think.

Rolo jumped back in, "So many people can quote musicians and movies but we want to know your thoughts about you *from* you."

One by one, youth shared what culture they're from, what religion they were; others shared if they were a brother, or sister, but when one of the youth said they were a student Dennis jumped up again and yelled, "Student of what?"

The girl was laughing, "I don't know. I'm in school so I'm a student."

Rolo yelled, "What school do you go to?"

We were all cracking up, as she pushed the name of her school out through her laughter.

Dennis yelled, "Is life a school?"

"I guess so," she said.

Rolo jumped back in, "You guess so? Every day, every opportunity, and everywhere is a school. Everyone is a teacher and a student."

"There are two types of teachers," Dennis said, "those who teach us *how* to be and those who teach us how *not* to be, but they're *all* teachers."

My first impression about those guys simply was that they were a trip. When I say they yelled it wasn't an I'm-stronger-than-you type yell. It was a we-are-actually-excited-to-be-with-you-and-to-be-alive type yell. It was cool and I liked their questions. They were going back and forth like they had been working together for years.

Rolo asked me, "Carlos what do you see yourself being seven years from now?"

I was playing the role right. Just because those dudes seemed alright I wasn't about to get into that talk. I shrugged my shoulders and said, "Nothing."

Dennis and Rolo looked at each other and started laughing.

Rolo looked at me, "That's pretty much impossible since you were already created."

Honestly I didn't get it then, but I kind of laughed out of nervousness.

What really caught my attention was when Dennis said, "Straight up, you guys are our heroes."

I was twelve years old and had been told over and over again by adults, some police officers, and even other kids I wasn't going to amount to anything. I was informed I wouldn't get out of our neighborhood unless it was in a body bag, going to prison, or joining the army. Which clearly shows another assumption was that I was looking to *get out* of our neighborhood. I loved my neighborhood and still do.

There I sat on my first day of the program listening to guys that were twenty-something and thirty-something years old speaking to youth without judgment and ignorant assumptions. Then they told us that we're their *heroes*. My head was spinning. It was my first day so I didn't want to ask the question I was thinking, but someone else did.

A girl leaned forward in her chair and asked, "Excuse me? How can we be your heroes? A hero is someone who helps someone else. You're supposed to be helping us."

Rolo and Dennis started laughing loud. The only reason us kids laughed was because of their laughs. Their laughter filled the room as well as our hearts. Some of us had already forgotten how to laugh for the right reasons or just no reason at all.

"True, we're here to help you," Dennis answered, "but if a day goes by where we don't learn something from you then we aren't doing our jobs."

Rolo softly added, "You're already teachers, cops, firefighters, lawyers, business owners, counselors, spiritual leaders, authors, musicians, Moms and Dads. Until the day comes when you see your dreams come true we will see them in you and for you. We're not here to look at you like your *just* kids. We're here to know what your dreams are if you share them with us. We'll do whatever we can to help you live your dreams. Even if you don't believe in you *yet*, we already do."

Dennis went from loud and excited to serious and gentle. "All of you no matter what you say or how you act are already our heroes because you've already had many reasons you could have turned your backs on hope, but you didn't. People turn their backs on hope over one disappointment or setback. Many of you already had several disappointments at a very young age, yet you still believe. You still want a brighter future for yourself, your family, and our community. That's just a *few* reasons why you're our heroes."

That was my first day of the after-school prevention program. It was nothing I expected. I was taken back by it all. I'd been around men their age that ignored me, threatened me, tried to recruit me, or left me. I'd been around men who expected me to comply with orders, or accept unfulfilled promises. Until that day I'd never been around men who told me I was their hero. I wanted those guys and the program to be *exactly* the way they presented, but after all I'd experienced they were going to have to prove themselves. I thought *they're full of it. I'm going to test them out and see if they're real.*

Monday through Thursday I would get picked up after school and go to the agency. I would disrespect the staff every chance I had. I laughed at the things the youth staff said. If they told me to join the circle I would go to the bathroom. Dennis,

Rolo, or Cody would have to find me. Every time I got pulled

aside by one of the youth staff they would ask me if I was

alright. All I would say is, "Yeah." The youth staff had to break

up several fights I got into with other kids. They would do peace

mediations between me and the kids I fought or almost fought.

It got to a point where one of the youth staff was assigned

to just me for the entire time I was at the agency. One of the

youth staff and I away from the group would play basketball,

throw a football, or walk around the block. While we did these

things they would try to get me to talk with them. They asked

questions about my life that I wouldn't answer. When they

realized I wasn't going to talk with them, they kept talking. The

whole time we were together they told me I was intelligent, I had

a bright future, and I was a blessing to the program. The more

they talked that way to me the angrier I became. I didn't show

them I was angry I would just say some rude things in the middle

of their talks, but that never broke their flow.

When I acted out at school the way I did at the program,

the reaction by some teachers was routine. I was told my

behavior was unacceptable, and I was wasting the other student's time as well as my potential. Next I was kicked out of class and suspended. The threats weren't threatening. The insults masked as *reverse psychology* is what I thought people at the school really felt about me, but were too scared to say straight. Attempts to make me feel guilty were futile. How can you make someone feel bad about their behavior when they already feel bad about their own existence?

I was hurting deeply. That's why I was hurting myself and others. The only people I didn't want to hurt were my mom and little brother. I had already seen death, gunshots, and gang fights. My dad was in prison and I didn't know *exactly* why. I had all those things going on in my life yet most adults couldn't look beyond the symptoms of my grades and behavior in order to see the cause of those symptoms.

I knew the youth workers at the prevention program saw the causes of my behavior. Some of the things they said to me during the few weeks they placed me in one-on-one time was exactly what I felt and been through. When I realized they *saw* me I was even more uncomfortable. I did what many do when the wounds are being touched. I was either real quiet or lashed out. I mostly lashed out.

After a few weeks in the one-on-one time, the youth staff transitioned me back with the group. I participated in all the activities but my sole mission was to mess up the program. I started interrupting, cussing, banging my hat to the left or the right, clownin other kids and the staff. I have to give it to the staff, they always tried to correct me and that's when I really showed out. I questioned them, asked them who they were to tell me anything and told them I didn't have to be in the stupid program. Yeah I turned it up for weeks. I pushed and pushed until finally I got what I wanted…a reaction.

During one of our group circles a girl was talking about how much it hurt because her mom was in prison and her grandfather was raising her by himself. She was crying and all messed up about it.

I started laughing and said, "This is stupid."

I had my head down and the whole room got quiet.

Before I even looked up Cody barked, "I think we've taken enough of your interruptions for as long as we can. Everybody here has tried to help you and you still have no respect for the group, the agency, or the other youth in this program. You're right you don't have to be here. You know where the door is."

I got up and started to walk out. As I was walking I realized I didn't want to be kicked out but my pride wouldn't let me change course. The last thing I heard Cody say while I was walking towards the door was that he was sorry this important topic got interrupted. He told the girl I laughed at to continue talking.

I started walking home and it was at least a two mile walk to my house. I found some reasons to feel proud of myself while I walked. One of the reasons I found was that there was this guy who always had it together and I finally found his button and pushed it. Walking home I thought *he's just like the rest of these lying, two-faced, fake people who aren't nothing but hypocrites.*

When I got home my mom and little brother were at the house. My mom had the night off from her second job. She asked me why I was home early. All I told her was that I got kicked out of the program. My mom wanted to know what happened. I wished she had left me alone. I told her the youth workers were fake and didn't understand me. She said she was going to go to the agency and talk with them. I told her it was alright because I didn't want to go back anyway.

We sat down to dinner. It was quiet. Mom was tired and no one spoke. After dinner my mom began washing dishes and I was playing a video game when someone knocked at the door. I looked outside and saw it was Cody, the same dude that told me to leave the program. I opened the door and he asked if he could talk with me and my mom. I got my mom from the kitchen, she let him in and we sat at our table.

I just knew that he was going to try to get me in trouble with my mom. Calmly he sat down at our kitchen table and revealed, "I'm here to apologize because I lost my temper today with you Carlos. I should have never asked you to leave the program because the program belongs to the youth. It belongs to you. What got me upset is how the girl in the program was spilling her heart's pain out about her mother being in prison and you laughed at her."

Right then my mom jumped in, "Is that true Carlos?"

"Yeah but..." I couldn't even get the rest out.

My mom yelled at me, telling me I was disrespectful and asking me how I could even think about laughing at someone when they're sharing painful things like that. It wasn't just what my mom said to me. It was her disappointment in me that messed me up more than anything else.

"Relax," pleaded Cody, "I'm not at your house to have any more yelling happen today. I simply wanted to apologize to both of you for losing my temper. Carlos, I think the reason you laughed at her is because you directly felt her pain. Her situation is almost the same as yours and that made you feel very uncomfortable."

My mom insisted, "Carlos you need to go back to the program and apologize to that girl. Cody is right. You laughed at her because her story *is* your story and that hit a nerve with you. Do you see that?"

I shrugged my shoulders. "I don't know."

"Carlos, you're welcome to return to the program. You still belong there. I hope you accept my apology and come back. You just think about things and do what's right for you. Regardless of whatever decision you make be true to yourself."

I didn't say much while Cody was at my house. I wasn't sure how to feel about the whole thing. What I did know is that was the first time I ever had an adult apologize to me.

The next day at school I saw some of the other kids from the program and told them, "I got that dude to apologize to me."

"What? Who?"

I was telling them how the youth counselor Cody came to my house and apologized to me for how he talked to me. I thought they were going give me some props for how I played it. They started telling me I should have apologized to him for the way I acted. Next they told me how much he had helped them and their families. I was just looking at them thinking, *you're sticking up for this guy*? Then they told me I should apologize to the girl I disrespected and how wrong *I* was.

I couldn't believe it. I felt confused, rejected, and corrected all at the same time. My own friends weren't giving me any props for how I finally got Cody mad.

All I could find to say was, "You guys got soft on me."

They shook their heads.

One of them said, "Carlos don't you don't get it? In the middle of everything we live through we finally have a place to have fun, be safe, and learn things from some pretty cool adults. Get your head out your butt Carlos and realize what we finally have is what *you* said, *you* wanted!"

I was dazed. My friends checked me hard. The bell rang and we all walked to our classes. I could have heard those things from any grown up and I know I wouldn't have listened, but these were my friends. Some of the same friends that helped me mess with other teachers and school counselors. Now they were sticking up for a girl in the program and an adult.

All day at school I kept thinking about what my friends, my mom, and Cody said to me. I thought *if I do go back to the program will I feel embarrassed? Does going back mean I lost this battle? I think I won because Cody apologized to me. I want to hang out with the friends I have in the program. I do like some of the stuff we get to do.* By the end of the day I decided to go back to the program. After school I got on the agency bus that took us there.

When we got to the agency Cody called all of us in a circle. I was thinking *he's going to yell at me or start giving us a speech about how we need to be respectful and blah, blah, blah.* I just sat back and was ready to get into ignore mode.

Cody started the circle saying, "First, here in front of everyone I want to apologize to you Carlos. I could have handled things differently yesterday. You all have to understand when adults make mistakes many times they try to hide the mistake. That's one of the reasons why people are losing the skill of finding solutions. Instead of admitting a mistake was made and seeking solutions people get lazy and hide it. That's also why youth learn to not admit or share mistakes because many times you just get criticized. Worse, some of you are beaten for mistakes. That's part of the cycle we'll break together. I don't believe in mistakes. I believe in the teachings that come from them, opportunities to learn and grow. Thank you all for teaching me so much yesterday. Carlos, I want to thank you for accepting my apology yesterday and for teaching me as well."

I knew bull crap when I saw it or heard it and I knew he was being real. It amazed me that an adult apologized to me. It set me at ease with the program and being back. Later on that day after the group Cody and I walked over to some tables that weren't being used by anyone. He told me that if I ever needed someone to talk with he would listen. I wasn't ready to say anything to him but I knew he meant it. He told me that I didn't have to carry pain alone, and the other youth workers were there for me when I was ready.

Cody ended that little talk by asking, "Is everything cool between us?"

I shook his hand and said, "Yeah."

It wasn't threats or guilt that drew me back. Love, in the forms of acceptance, forgiveness, and understanding brought me back. I saw the same love given to my mom with the attention and help she needed from the program she was part of at the agency. My mom would go to a parenting class once a week when she could. She wasn't crying as much and started to get a look back in her eyes, a sparkle I hadn't seen since my dad went to prison.

Dad, Introduce Me to My Family

I jumped into the program, got involved in what was going on, and wanted to be there. I went after school Monday through Thursdays. We played chess, had circles and talked about our lives and things we wanted to do. We played basketball, foosball, made music, watched movies and *yes* did our homework. I had no idea how much fun youth programs were. Within a few weeks of applying myself in the program I was doing better in school. I wanted to do well in school so the youth staff at the agency would be proud of me. After they told us we were their heroes I began wanting to live up to that.

After I had been in the program a few months the school year was coming to a close. Summer vacation was only a couple of weeks away so I asked Cody if there was going to be anything happening during the summer, or if we had to wait until school starts.

"Thanks for reminding me Carlos," He yelled out to everyone, "Gather around and listen up. I want to explain something to everyone before summer vacation starts. For those of you who don't already know we will be having a summer program for you guys. There's room for one hundred and fifty kids this summer. The summer program is six weeks long. Every week is a different topic we will learn about. Every Friday is a different field trip. We will end the summer program with a weeklong camping trip three hours north of here."

Everybody wanted to be part of the summer program. I wanted them to pick me and the friends I got along with best to be part of the summer program. I had to ask Cody if I was going to be able to be part of the summer program, I couldn't wait.

"Am I going to be able to be part of the summer program?"

"Carlos, all of the staff has a certain number of youth we can select to get a total of one hundred and fifty kids. You're my first pick if you want to be part of it."

"Of course I'm your first pick homie. I mean of course I want to be part of it Cody sir."

We both laughed.

"Seriously, I'm very proud of you Carlos. You have to know you've come a long way in a short amount of time."

I almost started crying because I was so happy. That was the first summer I actually had something to look forward to.

When I got home I told my mom about the summer program. She was excited I was going to have a summer instead of being at different people's houses during the day, and going home to sleep at night. I'm not sure who was happier, my mom or me. It was nice because we felt good again. It had been a while since we felt good.

After much anticipation the day finally came when the summer program began. It was like the after-school program but a lot better, longer, and more intense. Every week there was a different topic we learned about; team building, substance abuse prevention, violence prevention, HIV/AIDS and STDs prevention, other cultures, and every Friday just like they said we went on a field trip. The field trips were sweet. We went to the beach, laser tag, wave pools, museums, and baseball games.

The youth staff brought in guest speakers every week who would talk with us about different experiences. Professional athletes, musicians, police officers, ex-gang members, victims of shootings; you name it and they came in and talked with us. Every morning for six weeks Monday through Friday the agency bus picked us up. We had a great time. The best part was yet to come and I didn't even know it. I had no idea that summer could have gotten any better but it did.

After the six weeks of the summer program at the agency there was a one week break. After the one week break all of us had to be at the agency at six a.m. with enough clothes for five days, a sleeping bag, pillow, and all of our bathroom stuff. We showed up excited. Some of us had never been camping before. Some of us had barely been outside of our neighborhood. We didn't know what to expect but we were just ready to have fun.

We hugged our parents or whoever dropped us off and got on the bus. It was a three and a half hour drive from the agency to the camp. About an hour into the drive I saw more trees than I'd ever seen in my life. We finally got to the camp and there was nobody except us kids, the staff, and wide open space. We stepped off the bus and saw cabins, a lake, circles where people had campfires, a rock climbing wall, a ropes course, and a zip line. I took a deep breath and thought *we're really here? This is really happening, and we're going to be here for a whole week?* We all separated into groups with the youth staff and went to our cabins.

After we got our cabins organized we went to the cafeteria and sat at the tables. The youth staff from our agency and the camp staff were in front of all of us kids. Everyone introduced themselves and reminded us about the camp rules. We really liked rule number one, which was to have fun and enjoy being a kid. We were all ready to do that. The camp staff told us that we would be participating in horseback riding, canoeing, playing volleyball, softball, swimming, fishing, doing a ropes course, and having fires at night. After the camp staff explained the planned activities our agency staff told us to get ready to go swimming.

We couldn't get to our cabins fast enough to change and get a towel. Before we knew it we were at this lake that had a water slide and a big air thing where if you sat on it and another person jumped on the other end you would go flying up about ten or fifteen feet then land in the water. We slid down the water slide about a hundred times. We jumped around, got launched off of that air water thing by the youth staff and had fun, lots of fun. We stayed at the lake until it was time for dinner. We walked back to our cabins put our wet swim clothes up to dry, changed our clothes then went to the cafeteria for dinner. We all got in a line and ate so much food from the buffet we were feeling kind of tired.

In the cafeteria after dinner Cody, Rolo and Dennis let us know that we had some free time to either rest at our cabin or play some volleyball at the sand volleyball courts in front of our cabins. Some of us just chilled out in our cabins while other kids played volleyball. I just wanted to rest for a minute and maybe take a nap. I was lying in bed in our cabin with my hands behind my head and my eyes closed. I felt really relaxed and was thinking *I never knew a place like this existed. This is awesome.*

Before the sun went down the youth staff told us to go to the cafeteria to get some hot chocolate because we were going to sit around a fire. We went and made our own hot chocolate. We made it thick. There was more sugar and chocolate in our cups than water, but it was the best hot chocolate we ever tasted in our lives. All the guys were at one fire with Dennis, Rolo and Cody. The girls were at another fire with the female youth staff. We couldn't see the girls because the camp was so big.

We were sitting around a really big fire on benches made out of logs. We laughed about some of the things that happened at our first day of camp. Like this one kid Johnny who got launched from that air thing into the water by the biggest youth worker, Dennis. Johnny is a little dude so when he went flying up in the air he landed on his stomach and his whole body was red.

Some of the fellas wanted to know why the girls and the boys weren't together because the fire was romantic. The youth staff laughed and told us that we had plenty of time to talk with the girls away from the camp back in the neighborhood. It was nothing serious we were just talking, joking, laughing, and teasing each other.

Cody said, "Shhhh! Guys be quiet. Do you hear that?"

Most of us thought he was going to try to scare us and go into some ghost stories. We played along and were quiet.

"Well what do you hear?"

We were all listening and trying to hear *it*, whatever *it* was.

"I don't hear anything," one of the guys said.

"Exactly," said Rolo, "all you're hearing are the sounds of God. The air, the crickets, some deer walking through the woods, and the sound of this fire, doesn't it sound good?"

None of us answered. We just kept listening.

"What are we normally hearing in the neighborhood at this time of night?" Dennis asked.

Some of us answered saying, "Trucks, cars, planes, people yelling, glass breaking, sirens, some gunshots, lots of noise."

"Have any of you ever heard quiet before?" Cody whispered.

We all just slowly shook our heads answering no. The noise in my head cleared and the sound of the crackling fire became louder. We realized we had never been in the quiet before. Our version of quiet was going to our room, putting on some headphones and drowning out the sounds of the neighborhood with music.

Saying nothing Rolo slowly lifted his hand pointing his finger straight up until all of us were looking at the sky. In unison we all said "Whoa." There were so many stars you couldn't count them if you tried. They looked close enough to touch.

Rolo asked, "How many of you have seen this many stars before?"

Nobody answered. There was no answer needed. None of us had ever seen that many stars.

There we sat in God's noise looking up at heaven. We all stayed quiet to soak it in. Even if we wanted to talk there were no words to explain what we were seeing and hearing together for the first time. It was amazing. Like another world I only heard about on TV or the Internet. I don't know how this made the other guys feel. It made me feel small *and* significant at the same time.

One of the kids noticed that Dennis, Cody, and Rolo were tearing up and asked them, "What's wrong? Why are you guys crying?"

Cody wiped the tears away from his eyes. "We're not sad. We just never get tired of this and we love you guys a lot."

Listening to the silence we watched the sparks that floated up from the fire blend with the star filled sky. It looked as if heaven and earth were connected.

We finished our hot chocolates while the fire died down. Afterwards we went back to our cabins, brushed our teeth and went to bed. Most of the other kids were talking and goofing around while we were lying there. I couldn't stop thinking *this will be the first night in my entire life I'm going to sleep without all the noise I hear every day*. I felt peaceful, relaxed and protected all at the same time. I looked at the stars through the window of the cabin until I fell asleep.

The next morning I was awakened by the sun shining through the window on my face. Like The Creator's gentle hand waking me to let me know it wasn't a dream. We really were there and still had four more days of that awesome place together. I was the first one awake so I woke up the other kids. We took our showers and walked down to the cafeteria for breakfast. We had biscuits and gravy with eggs and orange juice, man it was good food.

During the next three and a half days we did everything they promised us and so much more. Horseback riding was one of my favorite things we did there. Most of us hadn't been that close to a horse before. We were a little scared but we made friends with the horses. The horse trainer explained to us that horses react to the feelings of the person approaching them. Most of us could relate to that type of horse sense the trainer talked about.

Some of the other stuff we did was a little scary, like the ropes course. We were thirty feet up climbing on those ropes going through the course while the staff and other kids cheered us on. It was scary but we did it. Some of us finished crying but we finished. We faced some fears together.

After the ropes course we talked about how it would be nice if when we faced something scary we had a group of people cheering us on. Some of us didn't have that back in the neighborhood. During that week we supported and encouraged one another like a healthy family.

Rolo, Cody and Dennis were like some big kids. They played everything with us and cheered us on when we felt nervous about some of the activities. I wasn't sure who was enjoying the camp more, the youth staff or us kids.

Every evening we sat around a fire. We talked about life, our hopes and dreams. A few times kids would share real personal stuff and cry. It didn't take long for us to realize we were all experiencing similar things within our families, schools and neighborhood. Realizing we were more similar than different brought us closer.

The last night of camp we were all brought into a building with a couple of really big tables. There were candles lit and soft music playing on a radio. The youth staff told us our last night at camp would be concluded with *letter night*. None of us knew what that was so we listened as Cody explained.

"Your parents, grandparents, guardians, whoever it is that cares for you, wrote a letter to each one of you. In these letters they are telling you how they feel about you. Tonight you're going to be reminded of how special and important you are from the people who love you the most. After you get your letters, take time to read them. Let it all sink in. *You are loved very much.* Even when it feels lonely you're not alone. There will be time later to read your letters aloud if you want to share."

I began thinking, *there's a lot of kids here whose parents had passed on, were deported, or in prison. Other kids are being raised by friends of their families or relatives. Some kids are raising themselves.*

Honestly, I thought Dennis, Cody, and Rolo made a mistake having letter night because a lot of us weren't going to get any letters. The youth staff began passing out letters. I noticed everyone was getting letters, several letters. Even the kids who I knew didn't have any family taking care of them.

When they gave me my letters I realized what was happening. I didn't just get a letter from my mom I got a letter from every single staff person in the program.

We sat there reading our letters. Most of us were crying while we read them. After we finished reading our letters we hugged each other and the staff. It was very emotional. Some kids read their letters aloud. One girl who got up and read a letter a staff person wrote couldn't stop crying while she read it. She was being told that she was strong and courageous. The letter was long and filled with compliments and observations of her greatness. I didn't understand how that many compliments could come from some of those youth workers. It would've been hard enough for me to write one of those letters to someone I really knew. That's when it hit me... *they really knew us.*

Despite our days of pushing limits, not listening or using bad language, the youth staff really knew us. No matter how hard we tried to keep them from getting too close they saw right through us. Many people don't really want to know another person; they want to know how they can get what they want from another person. I had heard about something called unconditional love but we were crying tears of joy because we *felt* it.

Along with a letter from my mom and little brother, I received many letters from the youth staff. I had to go outside a couple of times because I couldn't stop crying. I knew my mom worked two jobs and she did that out of love for my brother and me. I always knew my mom loved me. My mother always worked hard, gave me her time, and was concerned about my future. I always knew *how* my mom loved me. However receiving a letter she took the time to write explaining all the

reasons *why* she loved me, was completely different and very

important to me.

I needed a break so I went outside to read my letters a

second time away from everyone. Before I began to read them I

took a deep breath, looked up at the stars that blanketed the sky

and could hear the silence clearly. I read the letters again.

Reading each *I love you Carlos* and *I'm proud of you Carlos*, my

thoughts raced about my father, the sound of his voice and his

face. My mind and body were filled with thoughts and feelings

of my mother's hugs, my brother's laughter and friends that had

passed away from senseless violence. I was crying so hard it hurt

and was uncontrollable. I started to feel a sharp pain in my chest

and was back to the silence of that place. The stars were a

reminder of another world. I thought *there's so much I don't*

know and haven't seen yet. I want to live. I want to see more

things and experience more of what I experienced here, Life –

Living. As I was going through those emotions that sharp pain in

my chest began leaving. It was as if someone reached inside of

me and fixed something. Something I didn't even know was

broken, it was my heart. I sat quietly for a moment taking it all in and felt relieved. I remembered how Rolo, Dennis and Cody always said that real men cry. It might hurt for a minute but afterwards you feel good and it sure is better than living with a broken heart and bottled up poisons. I took another deep breath, wiped the tears from my face and went back inside. I listened as the other kids shared their letters but kept mine to myself.

After the letters were read everyone went outside to sit by the fire one last time together. We talked about the things we did at camp and what we liked best. The fire was big, warm and bright. At one point we were all just staring at the fire, nobody was saying a word. The only sounds were the fire, a soft breeze in the leaves of the trees, some crickets, and an occasional sniffle from someone. The difference between our last night and first night was we weren't uncomfortable with the quiet. As a matter of fact we liked it. I was already having bitter-sweet thoughts about going back to the neighborhood the next day. I missed my mom and brother, but I knew I was really going to miss that place and the times we had. It was one of the best things that ever happened to me.

The fire started to die down and one by one we went back to our cabins to go to sleep. It takes a lot to get a bunch of kids tired but we were. As I was lying in my bed I felt something I didn't remember feeling since my dad went to prison, it was *peace.*

The next morning we ate our last breakfast at camp together. All of us kids told the camp staff and the program staff thank you. We packed up all of our things and got on the bus. Most of us slept the entire three and a half hour drive back. It was good to get home, eat my mom's cooking and be in my own bed. I never realized how noisy our neighborhood was until I came back from a place that was quiet. I was lying in bed hearing car horns, yelling, tires screeching, people talking as they walked past the house, car radios and semi-trucks. I put my headphones on and listened to music to help me fall asleep. I really wanted to hear quiet again.

Dad, Introduce Me to My Community

After returning from camp I had two weeks before school started. I helped my mom around the house with chores and taking care of my brother. When my mom was at work and my brother was in day care I would read, play video games or talk to some of my friends on the phone. Sometimes my friends would come to my house and we played video games together. I was chillaxin. My mom wasn't getting any help from anyone, but she always found a way to take me shopping for school clothes one week before school started. I never got all the clothes I wanted but I got most of them. I looked good and I was in style. I was feeling great. It was a great summer.

The same uncomfortable conversation that always happened when my mom and I went school shopping happened again. I picked out some nice slip-on shoes. As usual when I picked the slip-on shoes my mom just looked at me and asked, "So, you're not ready yet?"

I smiled and answered, "Nope. Not yet."

My mom smiled and bought the shoes. I felt relieved because the couple of years before that year, she would try to have a conversation about it right in the store. I was doing well in school, at home and in the after-school program. My mom wasn't going to make a big deal out of my shoes like she had before. That took some of the pressure off.

Things were going too well for me to dwell on the only uncomfortable part of that summer. I wasn't going to let the part of buying shoes ruin anything for me. I was ready to get back to school. I was especially ready to get back to the after-school program, not just to be with my friends but to really move forward with my life. Before I went into the prevention program many adults told me to focus. The problem was I didn't really have anything to focus on. I finally had something to focus on, my future. No, I didn't know exactly what I wanted to do for a living or what I wanted to major in at college; but after that summer I was thinking about living and the possibilities of college. Simply put, I was introduced to some healthy thoughts and experiences that changed the way I was looking at things. My circumstances weren't changing, I was.

When school began I got involved in some positive groups in school and asked for tutoring in the subjects that gave me the most trouble. If I wasn't in school, studying, being tutored, or at the after-school program; I was at home with my mom and younger brother. My schedule was packed with things that brought me good feelings and good consequences. Looking back I can say I realized the world inside of me is as big as the world outside of me. I wanted to explore and find out more about both of those worlds.

Being hungry to explore those worlds with the guidance of healthy adults and friends was exciting. Put that on top of all the other things in my schedule and the years just flew past.

My eighth and ninth grade years were over before I knew it. I was sixteen years old and in the tenth grade. Over those years I stayed in the after-school prevention program, and was able to be in the summer program every year. It was some of the best times of my life. Things were good at home, my grades were all A's and B's, and I had a group of friends who loved me for me. We were all in the after-school program together. I was taking any and all positive advice from everyone who had some good things to share. I was looking into colleges and college testing study guides.

I was really only thinking about a community college or a vocational school until one day at the program Dennis talked with us about college and our futures.

"You young people from the neighborhood are doubly blessed. Never think you can't fit in somewhere, especially college. Those of us from the neighborhood do fit in college. Anyone can learn college routine and life, but not just anyone can come into our neighborhood and operate, live or function."

Even though Rolo was late for group that day he must have heard what Dennis was talking about because he peeked his head in the door and yelled, "You can operate in their world but they can't operate in yours."

He sat down and asked us, "Either on TV or on the Internet have you guys all seen a space shuttle launch?"

We all answered, "Yes."

Rolo continued, "The hardest part of a space shuttle launching is the takeoff. The shuttle has rockets on it that help it push through the force of gravity trying to keep it on the ground. The space shuttle was made to get into space. Without the help of the rockets it never gets to do what it was made to do. When the shuttle's rockets push it through all the forces that try to keep it down, the rockets break away because they're no longer needed. Healthy adults and friends are like those rockets on a shuttle. They're with you to help get you through all the forces that want to keep you on the ground. They help you push through the gravity of criticism, doubt, circumstances, fears, and tears, so you'll fly on your own."

That's what pushed me to push myself, because before I heard Rolo and Dennis say those things I did feel like I wouldn't belong in college. I thought about all the stuff I had seen and been through. I realized there isn't anywhere I don't belong. After that talk I started looking into schools in other parts of the country, scholarships and all that stuff. Honestly by my attitude and smile, people that knew me before really didn't recognize me. I had dreams and people who believed in me living them;

but that wasn't half as important as me knowing myself and knowing I can do whatever I want in this life. I felt empowered and knew I was on the right path.

I'm not saying I knew exactly where that path was leading me but even that was exciting. I knew where the path I had almost slipped down a few years before the after-school program would have taken me.

It may be strange to some, but if you've never been there try to relate to what I'm saying. If you don't have hope then you're not risking anything so it's safe. Even if how you're living will probably get you shot, put in a cage, or make you another statistic whose memory is short lived. Having hope and living you're dreams when all the statistics people accept are against you is much more challenging. Instead of accepting the statistics from the so-called experts, I accepted the challenge of living my dreams. I decided since everyone has to experience challenges, I was going to experience mine on the way to my dreams.

Within my environment were the voices of doubt and discouragement. When these voices mixed with feelings of jealousy and the consumption of alcohol and other drugs the actions of insane violence were born. Many men learned to abandon their dreams, dignity and children that *were* born from them; I hoped and prayed those same men would learn to abandon their false prides, fears, violence, alcohol and other drugs that *weren't* born from them.

I wanted the men in my community to remember who they were. To return to the reason they were born and what is supposed to be born from them. I stopped seeing the men in my community that were in their twenties, thirties, forties and fifties doing the same things they did when they were teenagers as losers. I began seeing them as wounded men whose hope had walked out their door. More often than not, the hope that left was in the form of their fathers. Like the space shuttle launch Rolo explained to us, their fathers were the rockets that were supposed to push them into flight. When their hope left, just like a space shuttle without rockets they remained behind, missing the most important piece needed for their journeys.

I'm grateful I allowed another person to be that rocket on my shuttle to help me launch. Of course I always wanted my dad to be the one who taught me. My options were to not launch or take the help of others and see what life was about beyond imposing perceptions of those who saw me as a problem or a victim. I didn't want to be another abandoned space shuttle sitting around for the rest of my life. I wanted to break the negative cycles for myself, my family, and my community.

I had the best of both worlds. I had my positive friends; most of them were in the after-school program with me. They were either hanging at my house or we were at their house. Then I had other kids who still talked to me, lots of times they would ask me for advice about their lives. There were youth who decided to be part of a gang that went to the after-school program but they didn't represent at the agency. It was funny how on the streets or in school they were enemies, but at the agency those same kids were doing team building, writing rhymes and kicking it with each other. I never said anything to any of them but it was cool to see. I liked seeing that because at that point in my life I liked peace. I couldn't drop my guard at most places but we all could at the after-school program. I think people who truly learn the importance of peace are those of us who have experienced the complete opposite. At times we have to dig deep to keep what we learn so it doesn't disappear in the chaos.

When things go that smooth for that long there's bound to be a challenge that comes along. Cody, Dennis and Rolo talked with us about that many times. They told us what we want to call problems are usually opportunities for spiritual growth. They would explain we are given opportunities to prepare, then opportunities to see if we prepared enough. As it always does, the day came when I saw if I was prepared enough.

The third week of my tenth grade year when I got home from the after-school program my mom let me know my dad would be coming back and be at our house the next day. I hadn't seen my dad since I was seven years old. I was excited, mad, and happy. I was all messed up inside. I didn't sleep well that night. I was lying awake in bed thinking about the next day with my dad. I thought about what he meant to me and what he had missed out on in our lives. I cried myself to sleep begging God to make things go good the next day for all of us.

The next day I went to school but all I could think about was my dad being at the house later. After school I stopped by the agency to talk with Cody. I really needed some advice. When I went in the agency Cody was about to run a group; I pulled him aside and told him I really needed to talk with him. As usual he made the time and got someone else to run the group. We went and sat down at a table.

Sensing that there was something serious going on Cody's look was that of concern, "What's going on Carlos?"

I took a deep breath.

"My dad will be at my house in a couple of hours. I'm excited but pissed off at him. I really want to see him but part of me wants to hit him. My relationship with my dad is the only thing in my life that's out of whack. Everything else is lining up for me. I always knew this day would come but I just kept pushing it out of my mind. More than anything I want my dad and me to have a relationship, a good relationship. He didn't want any contact with me, my mom or my brother this whole time. He told my mom that would make things easier on us. I think he was thinking about what would make things easier on him. You know, movies, ball games – that's the kind of stuff I want - it's what I always wanted. I'm angry and tore up inside."

"It's alright to feel all those feelings and to honor what's going on inside you. You can be mad at him and excited to see him at the same time."

I tried to let Cody's words sink in.

I murmured, "Yeah."

Cody suggested, "When you feel lots of things at the same time you have to put them in the right order. Take your time with this Carlos. You and your dad can't go through nine years in one night. Just focus on tonight, and remember all the skills you've learned to deal with life. Your dad is probably just as nervous as you are. His fear of rejection is no less than yours, just different reasons. Try to apply everything you learned with your dad, especially about communication. What are the rules you learned about communication?"

I said it without even thinking about it.

"If it's not with love, truth *and* to help then don't say it."

Cody smiled with gentle approval.

"Exactly, and you're talking about the truth because it's your feelings. Remember when you're going to tell him something, do your best to make sure it's with love and to help along with being the truth. If you guys want family counseling the invitation is open. Have your mom call or come by and we'll set it up. Let your dad know we're here for him too in case he wants some extra help in his transition back from prison. This is a big deal Carlos. Please stay close with us through this so we can be there for you."

I took a deep breath, shook Cody's hand and told him thank you. As usual he thanked me too. I told him I would let him know how everything went and that I would stay close with the youth staff through that challenge.

What I liked most about Rolo, Dennis and Cody is although they told us good things, they listened. I talked for at least an hour and Cody didn't say a word until I was done. The other kids and I knew they actually cared about us because they listened. Cody always said you can't truly listen to anyone if you're doing anything else. He didn't teach us by saying it he taught us by doing it.

On my way home from talking with Cody I had butterflies in my stomach. I didn't know what to say to my dad when I saw him. I got home and my mom had a big meal prepared on the table with four places set. There had only been three places on the table for years. Seeing the dinner table like that made me think *my pops is coming home, my dad, my hero*. I started to get excited and forgot about being nervous. I had so much to tell him about. How I was doing in school, the after-school program, my friends, what I'm thinking about studying in college, all of it. I hoped he was as proud of me as I was of me.

While I changed into some nicer clothes for dinner with our whole family I had thoughts of how my family would be

better and stronger united. The last time I remembered feeling
that way was when I was seven years old...

> *I sprung out of bed and my first thought was, my dad! I*
> *ran in the bedroom to wake him up so he could help me*
> *tie my shoes and go play baseball or something. When I*
> *went into the bedroom my mom was sitting on the edge*
> *of the bed crying and my little brother was in the crib*
> *next to their bed. "Where's dad?"*

> *My mom said, "Son, come here," She hugged me real*
> *tight. "Your dad had to go away for a while. Your dad*
> *isn't going to be back anytime soon but he'll be back. He*
> *didn't want to say goodbye to you because he didn't*
> *want to make things hard for you."*

> *I pulled away from her and yelled, "Who is going to*
> *teach me to tie my shoes?!"*

> *"Son, I will teach you how to tie your shoes and we'll be*
> *okay until your dad gets back."*

"He promised he would teach me to tie my shoes!
Nobody else can do that for me, only him!"

I pushed that memory out of my mind and decided since my dad is coming back everything will be fixed. I stopped feeling mad or sad, just excited; like I did when I was seven years old before I found out my dad went away.

I waited on the couch with my little brother and Mom. We waited and waited and it was starting to get late but I never doubted. I learned from Cody, Dennis and Rolo what a real man is so I knew my dad would keep his promise. Although we went a while without him in our lives he is a man, my dad and my hero regardless of anything. My mom, little brother and I sat down and ate because we had to go to sleep soon. We stayed up and watched the eleven p.m. news in case my dad got to the house before it was over. The news was over and my dad hadn't shown up. My little brother and I went to bed. My little brother and I stayed awake for a while just listening for a knock at the door, so we could run downstairs and hug him but that didn't happen either. We both fell asleep with our stomachs full but our hearts empty.

The next morning I went downstairs and saw my mom sitting on the couch smoking a cigarette which she only did when she was worried about something. I hugged her and as I began to ask her what was wrong, she looked at me with tears welling in her eyes and said the last words I wanted to hear.

"Your dad came by late last night and left some things by the door for the two of you but he isn't coming back."

Panic began to settle on me.

"How can that be? We're his family. You're his wife and we are his sons. That's not true, it's not true!"

"Carlos, honey it's not your fault or your brother's fault. It's my fault because I can't make him happy anymore so he found another place to be."

Full of anger and pain I just hurled out the words.

"You're right it *is* your fault, everything is your fault."

Those words haunted me the second I said them. I knew
it wasn't her fault. The only thing she did was support my
brother and me with unconditional love. I don't know why the
people we love the most and that love us get so much of our
negative emotional outbursts. While the people that really do
need to hear the truth about how they stepped away from their
responsibilities seem to be out in the world enjoying life while
the people they left behind suffer.

At that moment if he had been in front of me I could
have and would have knocked him out. All the years of
disappointment, hurt, and confusion converged into focused
anger. In retrospect, I'm glad he wasn't in front of me. Honestly
what could I have done to him that could possibly be worse than
what he was doing to himself? I was so upset about that
happening because it was on his terms. He wasn't being sent
away, he was back. He chose not to see us. I could've even
understood him not wanting to be with my mom, but choosing to
not be with his sons was something I didn't understand. I
couldn't put any of it into something logical because there was

no logic. At that moment the only thing that made sense to me was my hurt and the anger that always comes with it.

In an instant I felt hopeless, unwanted, and broken. Just the day before I was focused and sure about everything like I had been for several years. In one morning I felt like I was back at the beginning. A hurt, confused, seven year old kid just wanting his dad to love him but he wasn't there.

I didn't make it to school that day. I walked around the neighborhood thinking, *forget everything and everyone.* As I walked I thought about how I hated my dad and my life. I asked myself, *what's the point of having dreams anyway?* I sat in a park several blocks away from our home and yelled at God.

I told God a lot of things but one of the things I told Him was that I was done trying to do the right thing because nobody else was. I was so angry. The only person I wanted to take it out on said he's not coming around anymore, so I blamed God. After I vented to God about my feelings I walked around the neighborhood some more.

I walked with a feeling of loneliness so strong I felt a cold shiver up and down my spine. After a while I saw some of the same guys that would ask me for advice about life hanging out by the store skipping school. I said, "What's up" to them. Since I was skipping school too we walked back to the park and were hanging out. They were talking about smoking a blunt and asked if I wanted to smoke out with them.

"Nah, I'm good," I told them.

They passed the blunt around while we just kicked it about life. I wasn't going to tell them about what was going on with me but that blunt was tempting.

As soon as they started smoking it they were happy. They were laughing about everything and nothing at the same time. Every time it passed by me I thought about trying it because I wanted to feel like they were feeling. I wanted to feel happy.

You know what stopped me from reaching out for that hollowed out cigar with marijuana inside it? Every time I was ready to say "forget it, let me hit that," I kept hearing Dennis'

voice say, *every choice changes our entire life, making it better*

or worse.

About a year before that day Dennis was talking to us in

a group about how we all have a natural GPS system that keeps

us on the right path. He explained, "When a missile is sent

somewhere it constantly adjusts to make sure it's moving in the

right direction. Without adjusting it won't get to the target. Even

if it's off by a half of a degree when it's launched it will miss the

target by hundreds of miles. Our choices in life are like that.

Each choice we make is a readjustment to stay on target or one

that will take us many miles away from the dreams in our hearts.

Everything matters, whether it's a missile, driving a car, a plane,

or our walk through this human existence. The stops we make,

and the detours we accept all change the course of our life."

Dennis ended the group that day by saying very sternly

and loudly, "Every choice changes our entire life, making it

better or worse!"

It wasn't just what he said it's how he lived that influenced me. Dennis, Rolo and Cody became important people in my life, so their insight and conversations were important to me. As upset as I was and as much as I wanted the pain to go away I trusted what Dennis said. I trusted what he said more than the temporary fix of getting high, and the little bit of pressure from some other kids my age to get high with them.

After Dennis' voice kept going through my mind I decided to go home. I walked in my house, sat on the couch and felt good I was able to have at least one victory to chalk up for me that day. I was just thinking about things as I started to calm down. I looked to my right and saw the bag my dad left for me and my brother. I went over, grabbed the bag and opened it. My brother had already taken what my dad brought for him. I reached inside the bag and pulled out a box. It was a shoebox. My dad brought some shoes over then left us. I started crying and threw the shoebox across the room and walked out onto our front porch.

I was on the porch crying and didn't even notice our neighbor Janette was on her porch. When I heard her voice it startled me.

"Carlos, I talked with your mom this morning after you left the house. She told me about your dad coming by and leaving. I'm sorry that happened to such good young man like you."

I thought *Janette is cool. I always liked her and I really need to talk to someone.* I was getting ready to tell Janette about how I felt. Then Janette started telling me about how her mom left her, her sisters, brothers and dad. It was this big long story about her life and how devastating it was to her. She finished the story as she walked back into her house saying, "So I know how you feel and if you need anything just let me know."

I thought *how do you know how I feel? First, you didn't ask me how I feel so I could tell you. Second, you didn't even give me a moment of silence to speak. Third, you're talking about something that happened to you thirty-eight years ago. I just went through all this a couple of hours ago. Do you even remember how you felt?*

I didn't say any of those things I just thought them. Not because Janette went back inside the house but out of respect. I understood most adults don't understand how to listen to youth. Janette's response was frustrating but it was typical. I went back inside our house and picked up the shoebox I threw across the room. I brought it over to the couch, sat down and opened it. It was a new pair of shoes.

I looked down at the shoes I had on my feet. They weren't bad, just worn out from running all over the place. I wished there was someplace to run from what I felt at that moment but there wasn't. An ultimate need had been so close to manifesting then stripped away. Like a bolt of lightning at night that lets you see everything for an instant then it's gone. I sat in the darkness of my mind staring at the new shoes hoping a flash of light would return so I could see. No different than I had done for so long before I went into the after-school program. I was always hoping the front door of our home would open and my dad would walk back into our lives carrying with him the light of

fatherhood. I reopened the door of my heart for my dad, along

with all the possibilities my imagination brought to me about our

relationship. It was slammed shut once again.

The shoes he brought over before he left became

symbols for me. The new shoes represented my dad's effort and

maybe that was as far as he could walk in this life. I was certain

my dad closed the door of his heart long before I was born. I

knew hardening myself would eventually hurt the people who

love me. I didn't want to hurt anyone, yet I didn't know how to

soften the feelings I was having from another disappointment.

That time I didn't even want to forgive him. I didn't feel like I

had a reason. At that moment even if I had a reason, the truth is I

didn't know how. I did at least plan on using my anger for

something positive.

I sat on the couch debating what to do with the new

shoes my dad bought me. *Should I throw them away? Give them

to one of my friends? Sell them to someone? Should I keep them?*

I decided to keep them. I realized the shoes weren't nearly as important as the steps I could take in them. I could take the steps my dad was unable to take. I could make the walk to manhood even if I had to figure it out on my own. Even if I had to do it angry, sad, and disappointed I would use those shoes to keep walking.

I put the shoes on and they were comfortable. They weren't comfortable enough to make me forget what they represented for my dad and me but they were nice. I stared at the untied shoes on my feet, for a moment I considered trying to tie them. I quickly thought to myself, *no that's his job.* I tucked the laces inside the shoes because I didn't know how to tie them. My mother was the only person who knew about me not knowing how to tie my shoes. I was sixteen years old, so of course I could've learned how to tie my shoes. I could have taught myself in a couple of minutes. It was a choice. I chose not to learn to tie my shoes and I wouldn't let anyone else teach me. Perhaps that's the most significant part of my story.

Dad, Introduce Me to My World

A couple of months before my dad went to prison when I was seven years old I had a pair of shoes with laces. I couldn't tie them. It looked easy when I watched adults do it. I would try by myself but couldn't get it. It frustrated me so much I would cry. I wasn't frustrated because I felt like I needed my shoes tied. What was important was my dad being proud of me. I thought if I could tie my shoes he would be proud. The loops, the knots, all that stuff looks easy to someone who knows what they're doing; but at seven years old it was hard to figure out.

After some days of trying to tie my shoes on my own but not being able to I asked my dad to help me. He sat down, tied one of my shoes then untied it and said, "Now you do it."

I tried to do what I saw him do but couldn't tie them.

He got a little frustrated and said, "Just watch and do what I do." He tied my shoe again, untied it and said in a booming voice, "Now you do it."

I was shaking and crying while trying to tie my shoe. I kept apologizing while I was trying but I knew I was messing up.

My dad got really mad and yelled, "This is stupid."

He tied both of my shoes really tight to the point where it hurt my feet then he walked out of the house. He wasn't trying to hurt me that happened out of his frustration. I cried not because of how tight he tied my shoes. I cried because he wasn't proud of me.

I was looking for the day when I could say to my dad "Look, I did it." I asked my dad many more times to teach me to tie my shoes. He would always say "In a while" or "In a little bit." He was in and out of the house so much I never really knew when or for how long he was going to be home. After a while I stopped asking him but I knew he would teach me someday because he said he would.

My mom tried to teach me many times but I wouldn't let her. When she asked why I wouldn't let her I told her my dad will teach me, he's just busy right now. My mom and dad would get into arguments about him not teaching me to tie my shoes.

One night in particular I heard my mom yell, "Our son has been waiting for weeks for you to teach him to tie his shoes but you never did."

My dad yelled back, "Then teach him yourself, I'm busy."

"He doesn't want me to teach him. I've tried. He's waiting for you because you said you would."

There was a short silence followed by my dad's reply in a lower, almost defeated tone, "I'll teach him, back off and give me some space, I'll do it later."

I felt kind of important my mom would demand my dad to teach me to tie my shoes. I also felt like I think every kid feels; that my dad was the toughest, coolest, and smartest man in the world. He could teach me anything like nobody else. Waiting was alright with me because he would teach me when he wasn't busy.

As a kid I noticed it wasn't just my dad but all the adults would say they're busy. Even the adults I knew who didn't do anything but sit around and get high would say they were busy. At seven years old I thought *what are adults so busy with? And why do most of them look so unhappy even though they're busy all the time?* I still wonder why people forgot life is to be *lived* not merely endured.

I didn't know what my dad was busy with but it seemed a lot of people in the neighborhood knew. Once in a while I had adults come up to me and say things like, "Don't worry about your dad", "He's a big boy" or "Don't grow up to be like him." How can someone tell a youth to not worry about their dad? He is my dad and he'll always be in my mind even when he's not *on* my mind.

Those comments were frustrating and sad because of the impact our dads have in our lives even if we never knew them. Youth have adults telling them to be real and honest, but when it's about matters of the heart they get blown off. What some adults blow off are things they've been unwilling or unable to face themselves. You can only take someone as far as you've walked. That's why we can't find answers to many things, because people keep telling themselves and the youth to look the other way and pretend.

I was done pretending. If that meant going through some more temporary pain to get to a greater healing for myself and my family I was willing. No matter what we tell ourselves there's something in all of our hearts whether we admit it or not. Whether we talk about our dads in a good way, a bad way or a way that's indifferent he's in our thoughts. Our dads will always be with us no matter the emotions we feel or don't feel when we speak or think of them.

I planned to use the anger I had about my dad to keep walking forward. I had to do something positive with it, I learned that much. That's why I kept the shoes; why I didn't harden my heart, and part of the reason I chose not to learn to tie my shoes.

I still had to face my mom because I didn't go to school that day. When she got home from work I was expecting to get yelled at. My Mom walked in the house and instead of yelling at me for not being at school she hugged me and told me she loved me. She also told me the school called her at work and said I wasn't there. She told me she covered for me by telling the school I didn't feel well.

My mom looked at me with the soft eyes she always had no matter what was happening. "Son, I love you so much and even after what happened this morning I still don't want you to think poorly about your dad. Most importantly I don't want you to be like him in some ways."

I looked at her with tear filled eyes.

"Why does everyone say they don't want me to be like my dad? Is he that bad of a man? If he's that bad why did you get with him? Why would you have kids with a man you wouldn't want your kids to be like?"

"Son, I want you to know something. The young man you're choosing to be is the kind of man any sane woman would want her kids to be like. You can't control your father's choices

Carlos, only yours. I'm very proud of how you're choosing to be."

"I know I can't control his choices. I decided I'll use the shoes he left me to walk the rest of the way, the way that he can't. I'll do it for me and our family but I don't know if I can forgive him for this. It's happened one too many times."

"Forgiving him is for you not him. Please tell me you'll at least stay open to forgiving him when you're ready, on your time."

"I'm doing my best and I'll keep doing my best. Thanks for covering for me with school today."

I was about to walk away and go up to my room when the thought hit me, *my mom had just as much of a hard time last night and today as anyone but she didn't have anyone supporting her through it.* I turned around, walked back over to her and gave her a big hug.

While we were hugging I said, "Mom you didn't just cover for me with school today. You've covered me and my brother with your love our whole lives. Your love has been the strongest thing we have in our family. Thank you mom, I'm sorry about some of the things I said when I was mad. Nothing bad is your fault and I know my dad's choices are his."

While we were embraced I felt my mom's belly shake as she held back her crying.

My mom squeezed even more tightly.

"You have no idea how much I needed those words. You have no idea how much I needed this hug. Believe it or not son even adults who are doing their best don't have all the answers. God knows I wish I did, only so I could give them all to you. I forgave you for what you said to me the minute you said it. You were upset Carlos, I understand that. I love you."

"I love you too mom."

My mom pulled away from me, wiped the tears from her eyes and gave me a kiss on the cheek.

"Are you hungry baby? I can make something to eat."

"No thanks mom, I'm really tired, I just want to go sleep."

"Good idea son, I think we can all use some rest after today."

It was still hard to look towards my future as a man when the man I wanted to recognize me wouldn't or couldn't. I'm not talking about my dad seeing the way I looked, how I had grown and all those things. I wanted him to see me as an inseparable part of him. I continued to ask myself, *why won't my dad see me the way I see myself in him and through him?*

I went to bed and cried myself to sleep. I apologized to God for the way I talked to Him earlier that day. I begged God to take the pain away. I begged God to change my dad so he'd want to be in my life and teach me what he promised. I begged God to give me the strength to keep walking the good road because I felt like everything was closing in on me.

I woke up the next morning and felt pretty good. It was as if some of the weight of the previous day had been lifted from me in dreams I didn't remember. Maybe that's why sleep is important, so our spirits can go get what they need to continue this earth walk with the clarity it takes to stay focused on our purpose, the reasons we're born.

During those moments in all our lives where the torment and pain is so deep it feels like it will never end we have to hold onto something. I learned what I have to hold onto is inside of me not outside. The tiny burning ember left of a big bright fire almost put out by a storm can be used to build a bigger and better fire. In the worst of storms there's always a tiny bit of hope somewhere in the mess. No matter how dim it may be that small light will change the darkness and get us through. I had to stay focused on what I could see with my heart not my circumstances. I got dressed, ate breakfast and went to school. I was only out of school and away from the program for a day, it felt like forever.

Before the first bell I saw some of my friends that were in the after-school program. They told me Rolo, Dennis, and Cody asked about me the day before. They wanted to know where I was and they missed me not being there. I told my friends I didn't feel good so I stayed home. They asked if I was going to the program after school. I told them I would be going.

I was glad I had the program to go to at the end of that day. Knowing Rolo, Dennis, and Cody were asking about me made me feel better. They weren't our blood family but they paid attention. Even though they worked with anywhere between fifty to one hundred kids a day they still noticed I missed a day. Many kids in my community went unnoticed in their own homes.

Adults in some homes were keeping each other addicted. Others were trying to save one another. Some were busy just trying to survive. Everyone's entitled to their choices; however when choices of adults leave their children little options and on their own at an early age nobody will ever convince me those are good choices. I witnessed parents abandon their children for a bottle, pills, and a number of other things never leaving the sight of their children. I'm still not sure what's harder for youth. When they watch fathers vanish in front of them, or away from them.

I felt relief as soon as I walked into the agency. There were smiling faces telling me they loved me. The youth staff acted like they hadn't seen me in years. It was good to be at my second home.

Seeing Cody, Rolo and Dennis made me realize all that happened the day before wasn't over inside me. After a few minutes at the agency with my guard down I quickly started to feel about every emotion a person can feel all at once. It was like I was in a thousand pieces and trusted whatever they had planned for us that day could help me put the pieces back together.

Before coming into the program I had no place to drop my guard other than home so I usually just *got over it* or would *man up*. Two of many terms I now know are just code for *it hurts too badly to deal with* or *let's pretend and look the other way*. The saddest part about these and other lies of what a *real man* or *strong person* is supposed to be is that in one form or another someone else will have to deal with what we wouldn't. Chances are it will be those closest to us, usually the children. Youth carry the burdens of intergenerational trauma that cannot be extinguished by money, alcohol, drugs, being busy, or suicide. I didn't know it at the time but that day was the day I found out what could extinguish the intergenerational trauma youth carry for and with the adults in the community.

Dennis had all of us get a chair and form a circle. He told us he was going to introduce the topic for the day then the floor is ours for however and whatever we want to share about it.

"There are things others have done to us, and although it may have hurt we need to forgive them so we can heal. It isn't always about the person that hurt us. Many times forgiveness is an expression of loving ourselves enough to let go of the hurt others have inflicted on us. We can forgive people who didn't do what they were supposed to do. People who left us abandoned or who just didn't show up in our lives. The emptiness we feel from abuse or abandonment can be filled when we forgive."

I sat there thinking *I can get with that.*

Dennis continued. "I know we've talked about forgiveness many times. All the things you can think of that you already forgave or you think you're willing to forgive is good. Today let's take it up a notch for our own healing and growth. Think of the things you've put in the category of unforgivable. Should we forgive the unforgivable? Can we forgive the unforgivable? How do we forgive the unforgivable? The topic today is forgiving the unforgivable. The floor is open for discussion, comments, questions, and respectful disagreements."

There were only about twenty-five of us in the circle that day including Dennis and Rolo. For a couple of minutes everyone was quiet. Like me, some were probably hoping that topic was going to go away. Others were thinking about it and getting ready to say something. I wasn't sure if I wanted to stay or if I wanted to run.

A girl named Sarah was in the circle that day with us. She had been coming to the program off and on since she was in middle school. She was a senior at our high school and had a full scholarship to a really good university. She was a straight 'A' student and an athlete. She never shared much in our circles but always listened and liked to joke around with other youth and the staff. She was the last person any of us expected to break the silence on a topic like that but she did.

"Alright, the topic is forgiving the unforgivable, right?"

"Correct," said Dennis.

"So if something is unforgivable then how do we forgive it? It's unforgivable right? I guess I don't get it."

Dennis leaned forward in his chair.

"Great question, does anyone have anything to say about what she's asking?"

Again there was silence for another couple of minutes. This time Rolo broke the silence and asked us, "What are some examples of things that are unforgivable?"

Sarah spoke up quickly, only now her voice was shaking and tears were in her eyes.

"Rape, murder, abuse, molestation, just to name a few; there's more on my list of unforgivable that's just my top four."

Rolo empathized, "Those are horrible things I wish nobody has ever experienced or ever will experience. I have to ask a question. Have people forgiven things that horrible before?"

He was asking everyone in the circle but it was Sarah who answered, "Yes."

Dennis asked, "Are some things in and of themselves unforgivable, or do we as individuals place things in boxes of forgivable and unforgivable?"

Sarah broke down crying. It was strange for us because nobody had ever seen her like that. We all just saw her laughing, playing sports or giving good advice. Dennis handed her a box of tissues and asked her if she wanted to leave and talk with Cody one-on-one.

"No I'm alright. It's just that this is crazy. This past Sunday I was thinking and praying about this very thing. I forgave the man who did what he did to me and a few other girls on my block when we were kids. I forgave him because I know he's a sick individual and in prison. It's easier to forgive if you know the person is being punished somehow."

She couldn't hold it back. The current of her tears was too strong. It pushed her heart's pain out through the thin veil everyone has within us that separates pain and healing. Her tears and words became intertwined like the reflection of the stars on still waters at night, purifying the moment while illuminating all our paths.

"I forgave that predator a long time ago because I wasn't going to allow a sick, twisted person to ruin my life, but I hadn't forgiven my dad until this past Sunday. He left us when I was just a baby and I never saw him. I don't know where he is. I always thought if my dad had been with us that guy couldn't have done what he did to me. I blamed my dad for not being there for the good times and the bad. Every happy and sad moment in my life I asked the same question. Where's my dad? Things didn't work out with him and my mom, fine. Why leave me? What did I do? Why wasn't he there at least that one time to protect me? It sounds crazy you know? The unforgivable I carried around for so long wasn't for the person who violated me physically. It was for the man I never knew. The man inside my heart, the man I looked for in other men but couldn't find because I never knew him; my own father, who I just forgave the other day."

Sarah's tears began to subside and a glow slowly came from behind her beautiful tear filled eyes as she continued.

"I was thinking about graduation this school year and getting ready to have another event in my life ruined by my dad not being there. That's when it occurred to me. I was actually preparing to make a good day into a bad one because of my dad. I thought this is my time, my life and my future. I could pretend and say forget him and that he didn't matter but that would be a lie to myself. The only way I knew to get rid of this heavy bag I've been carrying around all this time was to forgive him. I'm not saying I didn't almost choke on the words *I forgive you*. It wasn't easy to say, but once I said those words I felt different. Like this two hundred pound bag filled with my dad I had carried everywhere with me was no longer necessary. I guess I just got tired of carrying it. I was tired of the anger and pain that always came with the bag. I reached out to The One who can do for me what I couldn't. I was given the strength to forgive and put the bag down. I learned that unforgiveness always comes with a bag to carry. The bag slowly grows heavier over time and eventually stopped me from walking my path. I figured since I've been strong enough to carry a pain around I let ruin most of my teenage years; I'm strong enough to forgive. The most important thing I learned is it takes just as much strength to either carry the hurt we have or forgive those who have hurt us. The difference is one frees us, the other imprisons us."

Her tears had stopped when she finished speaking but most of ours were still going. All of us got up, gave her a hug and let her know we love her. I hear a lot of people say things like *be real* or we need to have *real talk*, I understand the shallow meaning behind phrases like these. What and how Sarah shared was truly *real talk*.

Rolo looked at her and rejoiced, "Thank you so much for sharing what you did with all of us. It's truly an honor to be in your presence and witness a courage so many people don't use anymore."

Rolo paused for a moment, then asked her, "Are you alright to go on with this circle or do you need a break?"

She started laughing, "I'm fine now. I actually feel better after saying what I thought would kill me. There aren't many people in my life who I can share my heart with. Thanks for listening. Thanks for the time, support, and hugs. It means a lot."

She laughed again which made the rest of us laugh. We needed that laugh to go on with the reality of the realm within our hearts and minds we ventured into that day. I couldn't help but wish it was me who was on the other side of my pain, laughing a laugh of relief. Sarah reminded and encouraged me that sometimes to get to the clarity, laughing, and peace we have to take the walk she did.

We have to be willing to walk through the temporary pain with someone we trust enough to be vulnerable with. Other times we have to walk through those moments alone; if we never take that walk then we're like so many people standing on the battlefield of life, putting on a smile so others don't know we're wounded. Some people think this is *strong,* but silently suffering causes us to slowly bleed out unnoticed. Somehow we have convinced ourselves this protects us from further hurt. There are people willing to help who never know we're hurting, so we continue to bleed never understanding the possibilities of healing.

I didn't know when or for how long Cody was in the room where we were having that circle.

He was standing on the outside of the circle right behind me when he said, "Does everyone here realize Sarah shared she took the shortest walk a person can take in this life, but so few make?"

Cody smiled looking around the circle waiting for someone to respond. We were all pretty sure he knew we didn't have a clue what he was talking about.

After a brief pause he continued. "The shortest walk anyone will ever take in this life is only about seventeen inches. Few people make this journey because it requires what Sarah shared, it requires forgiveness. This very short walk is from our head to our heart. Sarah took that walk, found her healing, and was generous enough to share it with us. That's a walk so many people will never make because they're unwilling to forgive. You can't make that walk without forgiveness, and you can't reach your optimal potential without taking this walk. I can promise you two things. The first is that taking this walk isn't nearly as painful as not taking it. The second is once you take this walk you'll have new eyes to see. Hate becomes Love. Despair becomes Faith. Hopelessness becomes Hope. Selfishness becomes Charity. Talking about it is good but experiencing it is much better. Wouldn't you agree Sarah?"

Sarah smiled. "Cody is right. It's really worth it. It's a little scary and uncomfortable, but anything worthwhile means we have to go beyond what we already know so we can know something new."

Rolo started to wrap the group up. "Are there anymore comments, questions or concerns?"

The youth staff gave everyone a few minutes to say or ask something but nobody did.

Rolo said, "Before we leave the circle I want to end it with this. Forgiveness is what truly breaks the unhealthy cycles. For years I was filled with so much anger towards quite a few people including my dad. I learned my unforgiveness was the cause of the anger I carried. To paraphrase Nelson Mandela, I also learned the anger I carried towards people was like me drinking poison every day hoping the people I was mad at got sick. The only person getting sick from me drinking the poisons of anger and resentment every day was me."

The circle ended that day with an unusual quiet. Normally when our circles finished it got loud quick with the sounds of chairs, talking, and joking. That day it seemed like everybody moved in silence and slow motion.

After a while the other kids eventually got back to playing sports, pool, or talking with friends. I was sitting on a couch when Cody asked me if I wanted to talk. I didn't hesitate and said, "Yes." We walked to a room and sat down.

Cody said, "The topic today of forgiving the unforgivable makes you think doesn't it?"

"Yeah, that's why I want to talk with you. I got so much… Not as much as Sarah… but a lot of…"

I paused because I felt guilty. I thought about what Sarah had endured by a predator. I started to think what was causing me so much pain and setback in my life was easy compared to what she had went through. Thankfully Cody recognized what I wasn't saying. I'm really grateful that he utilized my pause to share what he did.

"Carlos, pain is subjective. If something is causing you pain nobody can say their pain is more or less than yours. You're the one that's feeling it not them. You know by now if it's important to you then it's important to me. You decide if you want to talk or not. My time is all yours right now, whatever you choose."

I was so jammed up with emotions from what happened the day before and in the circle that day. I didn't know where to begin. I remember thinking *what words do I use when I don't even know what I'm feeling?*

I decided not to bother with the words. I just let out what I was feeling. I didn't place importance on being able to explain it or not. Besides, some of the most significant things that happen to us in life have no labels to match the experience anyway.

When I first began to speak I only told him about what happened the day before. I started where I was at the moment and thought that was pretty much it. Then the rest just came out like a major leak in a damn. The wall I used to block my life from everyone all those years started to crumble. I told Cody about my dad, my sadness, and my confusion. He was the first person outside of my mom I told about me not knowing how to tie my shoes; and all the reasons I was waiting for my dad to teach me.

The entire time I was talking my mind kept telling me to shut up but my heart wouldn't let me. I cried so much while sharing my life and feelings with him. I explained how I spent years thinking if I could've tied my shoes, been better at sports or didn't spill things at the dinner table then my dad would want to be around me. There were so many years of pain coming out as Cody listened. I shared things I never talked about with anyone other than my mom. I also shared things I hadn't even thought about in a very long time.

I knew if I didn't talk with someone that day I never would. There are times when all the signs are guiding us to a moment we think will be uncomfortable at best or unbearable at worst. More often than not those moments are when we face ourselves. We can either ignore the signs or pursue them. I knew not following the signs of my path would eventually bring me more pain than following them.

After over an hour of talking I shared one last thing with Cody.

"I'll do my best to take that short walk you talked about in the circle. I don't think it will be easy, but I'm going to forgive my father. I'm just not sure how to do it."

After I was done talking Cody allowed the moment to settle in by working *with* the silence not against it. I appreciated that because it gave me a moment to realize I too was on the other side of some of my pain. Just as I had watched Sarah earlier move from tears to smiles. I was in a similar place simply by knowing a healed person then trusting the process of speaking from my heart. I felt good, lighter and a little tired.

After a moment of comfortable silence and realization Cody said, "Did you need me to just listen to you today, or do you want to talk about what you shared?"

"I feel really good after getting that out of me. I appreciate the time, and I'm open to having a conversation."

"First off you're very courageous to share your life story with me. I honor your courage and trust. You don't realize you already forgave your dad, and that you're already taking the walk from your head to your heart."

"What do you mean? I didn't think that…"

"What? That you could forgive him and still wait for him to teach you to tie your shoes, and sometimes feel mad at him?"

"Well, yeah."

"You already forgave him or you wouldn't be willing to wait for him. You're just mad and disappointed with him again. You've found the most ingenious way to forgive someone I've ever witnessed. You're walking forward on your path, and keeping your shoes untied in case he ever wants to catch up with you. You have the compassion to allow that particular thing to be only for him and nobody else. You have the patience only love provides for it to happen when your dad is ready. At the same time you're holding your dad accountable. You're not allowing anger to punish him. You're agreeing with forgiveness to make its own corrections in its own way. Once you let the reality of the path you've chosen sink in you'll be less harsh with yourself. You just taught me more about forgiveness than I could ever teach you."

"I never looked at it that way. I always thought not letting go of what he promised was not forgiving him."

I started laughing because I recognized I had forgiven him all along. I've always forgiven him.

"Pretty cool Cody. This is pretty cool."

"Yes it is pretty cool; as a matter of fact I think it's amazing. Sometimes when we're walking the road from our head to our heart we question if we're on it; not because we can find things we're doing wrong, but because of the words and actions of others. Keep in mind to always look at the intent of someone sharing a criticism. People who are walking the Sacred healing road you've been traveling may at times provide correction but not punishment. Correction always gives insight with encouragement to do something better. Despite the fact

correction may sometimes sting it's always with love and to

help. Punishment is always with fear and discouragement.

Punishment doesn't come from those walking the path you've

chosen. It comes from those who are unable or unwilling to walk

the path you've chosen."

"I'm not going to leave my path Cody. I didn't even

know I was on it. Now that I know I'm on it I have no plans to

leave it."

"Carlos, we all stumble on our paths. Most of us have

taken a detour or two chasing illusions; attempting to see if we

could run away from ourselves. Those of us fortunate enough to

return to our path after the detours see our true path with more

clarity. Be compassionate with yourself and others. Don't let the

negative voices within you or outside you take you off your path.

Thanks again Carlos. Thank you for teaching me so much

today."

After talking with Cody and getting a completely

different perspective on why I didn't tie my shoes it made the day before seem meaningful not meaningless. I thought I took

two steps back the day before. Had I given up, I never would

have realized I was *already* doing what I thought I couldn't.

When people talk about miracles they're often talking

about The Creator changing circumstances. When God changes

not having a job into having a job; not having food into having

food; not being able to pay rent into being able to pay rent. I

thought I was lacking something I wasn't. I thought I didn't

know something, but I did. I was offered and *received* the

correction which changed the way I looked at not tying my

shoes. Such a subtle change in my perception transformed

everything else I looked at for the better. At that point in my

journey there was no greater miracle.

Dad, Help Me Tie My Shoes

The Sunday after I talked with Cody my mom woke me up early. She thought it would be good for us to go to church together. We hadn't gone to church in years. My mom's work schedule didn't allow us to spend a lot of time together, so it was cool with me. The pastor of the church we went to was from the neighborhood. My mom knew him pretty well. I went to school with his kids. After the service we stayed and visited with some of our friends. During the visit with our friends, the pastor came up to me and asked if we could talk.

I looked at him and said, "Who?"

He laughed and said, "You and I. Can you and I go talk?"

I reluctantly said, "Sure."

We went over to some seats away from everyone else and sat down.

The pastor said, "I want to talk with you because your mom spoke with me last week. She is concerned about some things going on with you."

I remained silent. I felt betrayed and angry my mom talked with the pastor about me.

I watched as he geared himself up with a deep breath. "Your mother is concerned because of you refusing to learn to tie your shoes. She wants to make sure you're okay."

He paused and was looking at me. I wasn't expecting any of that. I was angry. It seemed like hours passed as I thought *the only people who knew about this were the people I wanted to tell. Besides, Cody and I already worked this out.*

Instead of him letting me get my thoughts together so I could respond, he felt the need to keep talking.

"I'm a pastor as well as a counselor and I'm concerned that you refusing to tie your shoes may have something to do with childhood trauma. The anger you carry about the trauma is sometimes a reflection of your relationship with your real Father, God."

He was making some pretty big assumptions about my entire life and what I was thinking. I knew who he was but he didn't know me. He never spoke with me before. What he said next really caught me off guard. Somehow it was also funny because of the breakthrough I had just days before.

"Do you realize your refusal to tie your shoes is an indication of your emotional growth being stunted?"

I paused for several minutes keeping both my anger and laughter under control. I took a deep breath through my nose and out through my mouth.

"I realize I'm sixteen years old and not everyone is going to understand my reasons for not tying my shoes. I have my reasons and they're none of your business."

"Would you let anyone else teach you how to tie your shoes?"

"Nobody other than my dad."

"Not even God?"

"Would you let God preach next Sunday and you sit in the crowd with us?"

"How would that work Carlos? I have to be up there to do my job because that's what God called me to do."

"That's how I feel about my dad teaching me to tie my shoes. It's part of his job that God gave him. If it's my turn to wash the dishes my mom won't let me make my brother do it. Why would I ask God to do something He already entrusted my dad to do?"

The pastor got a look on his face and I wasn't sure if he was angry, sad, or just thinking. He looked down at the floor then back up at my eyes a few times before he said anything.

"Carlos you know it wasn't until you just shared what you did with me that I fully understood a sermon I gave a few years ago titled, *God Holds Us Accountable Through Our Children*. It was a beautiful message I was given when I was deep in prayer. It really moved the whole congregation that day.

Part of the message of what God told me to share that Sunday was The Creator allows children to hold parents accountable for what they were asked by God to give their children. Many times when children hold parents accountable, parents get angry or completely miss the message. Your dad's emotional growth is stunted, not yours. You're trying to help him grow up. That makes you a teacher and a young man wise beyond your years."

The pastor sat for a moment looking around the room as if he was searching for something then abruptly asked, "Carlos can I ask you to do one thing for me?"

"What's that?"

"Will you at least share with your mother about where you're at? She's worried about you. After you and her have a talk, it would relieve her to know how far ahead of the game you are with this."

"We'll talk. This is really the only topic we avoid because she always sees it as a problem. I know what you're saying. We'll talk when the time is right."

I went from feeling angry and betrayed to feeling empowered. The pastor and I shook hands. I walked back to my mom, brother, and the friends they were talking with. After my mom was done visiting we walked to the car and drove home. During the ride home I didn't say a word about my conversation with the pastor.

When we got home I went to my room and chilled out for a little while. I was kind of laughing to myself thinking *did I just teach a pastor who is also a counselor something today? What a trip this world is when you let go of all the garbage and opinions of others and truly be who you were created to be.*

After about an hour I went downstairs. I couldn't wait for my mom to ask me about the pastor. She had more patience than me so I brought it up first.

"Why did you tell the pastor about me not wanting to tie my shoes? The only people I wanted to know about it were the people I told."

She had a soft look of regret. "Honey I'm worried about you. It hurts me to watch you holding on. Waiting for something you may never get from the person you want it from."

"Mom, I'm not waiting for him. I'm moving forward with my life. You told me to forgive him for me and that's the only way I know how to do it."

"What do you mean?"

"I'm walking my path in my shoes and moving forward. They'll be untied if he ever wants to catch up with me and fulfill his promises. I'm not leaving my path to chase him or anyone else. I'm leaving my shoes untied so I know if he has changed or not when he catches up with me. It wouldn't be forgiveness if one day he comes and offers peace and I reject him. It wouldn't be smart if I just let him back in my life because he uses some nice words masked to offer more disappointment and pain. The shoes are his to tie. They always will be. That way I'll know if I need to let him know I've always forgave him and keep walking forward; or let him know I've always forgiven him and allow him to walk with me."

My mom began crying and hugged me real tight. One of those *mom hugs* you never get too old for; the hugs we long for after they pass on. The hugs we want to feel again and sometimes do in our dreams. She pulled back keeping her hands on my shoulders as she looked in my eyes.

"Son you're a man now. You've grown up so quick and the way you're thinking is more than I have ever hoped or prayed for. I'm so proud of you. I apologize for telling the pastor about things. If I had known this is how you've been thinking I never would've spoke with him. When did you start looking at things like this?"

"I finally opened up to someone else about it. I talked with Cody. He helped me put things in a better perspective."

"We're blessed to have Cody, Dennis and Rolo in our lives."

"I know mom, trust me, I know."

"Mom, do you think dad would hold me accountable for things if he was with us, and being the man I know he could be?"

"I married him because I saw the man he could be. The lesson I learned is you can't have a relationship with someone's potential. You can only have a relationship with who they choose to be right now. To answer your question, yes, he would hold you accountable. That's one of many things good parents do."

"Well why did you worry about me all these years, for holding my dad accountable?"

"Honey, it's like you, your brother and I have been waiting to be put back together based on your dad's choices. We can only control how we live. I didn't want any of us wasting another minute of our lives living in anger or sadness because your dad won't step up. I know nothing is wrong with you. I apologize for telling the pastor about why you don't want to tie your shoes. I love you Son. I'm so proud of you. You're doing great. You're the man of the house. Even without your dad you've figured out how to be a really good young man with the help of some good men. It just sucks that you had to do so much of it on your own."

"I didn't have to figure it out on my own. You helped me as best you can. Something else the youth staff at the program taught me is there are people who teach you how to be and people who teach you how not to be. Almost everything I've learned from my dad about being a man is how not to be. Do you know how much it hurts to say that about my *own* dad?"

Tears welled up again in my eyes.

"I just want him to teach me how to tie my shoes. Is that too much to ask?" It was beyond words at that point. She didn't need to say anything. She held me and let me cry a little more.

The next day things felt so-called normal. I went to school then the after-school program. It was packed as usual. We ate some snacks and were visiting with one another. After we relaxed a while Cody, Rolo and Dennis had us all get a chair and form a circle for group. Dennis handed each one of us a pencil and a piece of paper while Cody explained what they were for.

"There may be some people in your lives you may never get an apology from. Perhaps they hurt you. There's a strong possibility we will carry that hurt around with us a long time if we don't get the apology we need or want. Today you're going to write a letter of apology to yourselves from whomever you need or want one from. We will have a discussion about this exercise today and tomorrow. Clear your minds, open your hearts, and go find a space where you can write."

We all went off by ourselves to different parts of the youth center. Most of us had no problem picking out the people we wanted apologies from. Writing the letter, now that's a whole different story. Writing an apology letter isn't as easy as it sounds. Those kinds of activities deal with the real and that's why we felt it. Some people aren't willing to feel the temporary pain which comes from that kind of self-work. We trusted the staff, so matter how deep and emotional an exercise was, it always made us feel better afterwards. Away I wrote...

Dear Carlos,

I may not ever be conscious enough in this lifetime to make things right. I may not ever be able to speak this directly to you. As you read this please hear my voice. I got caught up in this world. I lost focus of what's real and what being a real man means. It wasn't my intention. It's never a man's intention to push away the only good things in his life. I've been out all these years trying to prove my manhood to the world. This whole time I have a son like you who never questioned my manhood. As a matter of fact I'm your Hero regardless of my blindness. I became blind with anger, pride, and hurt. Most of all I became blind with fear. These things left me paralyzed. I couldn't be what I was supposed to be for you. I couldn't even be what I was supposed to be for myself. I wasn't able to forgive myself. I was hurting, so I attacked all the things that were beautiful in my life. I felt unworthy of goodness. My spirit knows the truth, but my spirit became smothered with substances that alter a person. Substances that turns people into everything they swore they would never become. I apologize for leaving you alone. I apologize for not hearing your needs or seeing your tears. I apologize for not teaching you how to tie your shoes. I know I should have cared for and cultivated your spirit. You're sacred

and you are truly a gift from God to this world. I beg you

to release the pain you carry because of my absence.

Use forgiveness for what it's for...to free yourself and

your children. Release me from the captivity of hate and

pain. Become the man I couldn't. Son, please forgive me

so you can be a man and servant of The Creator. I

apologize to you my precious son through this letter.

Begin your true journey taking the necessary steps along

the way. Become the man I wasn't strong enough to be.

Love, Dad

When we were finished writing the letters we went back

into the circle. Those of us who wanted to read our letter aloud

had the opportunity. Every time one of the kids stood up and

read their letters it was with tears streaming down their face. We

all felt one another's pain as well as the healing. Afterwards we

hugged each other. Most of us had the same letter just in

different words. There were more letters from dads than anyone

else.

Rolo said, "Thank you for everyone's participation. Do you have any thoughts about the fact most of the letters are from fathers?"

I didn't feel like sharing anymore than I already did. I just listened. One by one my friends in the program talked about how their dads weren't with them. The reasons varied. Some shared how their moms wouldn't let their dad come around, yet never explained why. Some shared they didn't know who their dad was. Others shared they never even seen a picture of him or knew his name. Others shared that their dad is at the house but he either doesn't say anything, or when he does, he yells.

After everyone who wanted to share was finished, Dennis said, "Raise your hand if you have your dad in your life?"

Out of all the kids in the circle that day only a few raised their hands.

Rolo inquired, "How many of you who have your dad involved in your life can say he is a good example of what a man is supposed to be?"

There were only three hands raised to that question. While sitting there I thought *where are all the men? Where do they go? How would they feel knowing their kids couldn't raise their hands to these questions?*

Cody stood up. Looked at the ground and shook his head. It was obvious he was regrouping himself before he spoke.

"Whether you accept the apology and forgive the person is entirely up to you. What I propose before you make the decision either way is this. Blaming others and ourselves just means we've accepted the dis-ease offered to us. The only medicine that can cure the pain that lingers after the moment has passed is forgiveness. Do you know what responsibility is?"

I said, "Yeah, it's doing the things we're supposed to be doing."

"Can you do things you don't know how to do?"

"No, not until we learn them."

"Correct! Response-Ability, response-ability is our ability-to-respond to life's situations. We can only respond with the abilities we've learned and cultivated. A very common ability people have learned and cultivated is blame."

Dennis jumped in, "Blame is a tool passed on to us from hands too wounded to pick up something different. The tool of blame only serves to build prisons of anger for ourselves and others. You can spend the rest of your life blaming yourself, your dad, or someone else for not being in your life."

Rolo chimed in as well, "Answer me this. How much blame will change anything that has happened in your past?"

We all said, "None."

"How much blame will change your future for the better?"

Again, we all answered, "None."

Rolo continued, "Forgiveness is not allowing people to walk all over you. Forgiveness is not allowing predators into your life. Forgiveness is not being a doormat. Forgiveness is not closing your eyes and ears to someone's negative intentions. Forgiveness is not saying *yes* to everyone. Forgiveness is not trying to make everyone happy. Forgiveness is not weak. Forgiveness is not blame. Most of you already know what forgiveness isn't. You've spent many years using the tool of blame. Has it made anyone in this room truly happy?"

I had to say something because I was getting frustrated.

"No, it hasn't made me happy. But what are you guys saying? Are you saying that nothing is anyone's fault? My dad leaving us isn't his fault? Somebody that murders someone in cold-blood isn't to blame for the murder? Where does it end?"

"It doesn't!" Cody said, "Forgiveness and blame are both limitless. Blame takes the painful moments in our lives and turns them into the rest of our lives. Forgiveness is the only action that can reach into our past, present, and future to bring us peace with it all. Nothing else can do that."

He paused, looked around the circle and continued, "Let me put it another way. If everyone who has deeply hurt us was on their death bed in excruciating pain with only five minutes to live, would you find it a little easier to forgive them?"

Most of us in the circle shook our heads motioning yes.

"Of course you would because in that position they're helpless and hopeless. There's nothing you can do to a person who chooses to bring pain and torment into other people's lives that's worse than what they're doing to themselves. People who spend their days sharing pain and hurt have never lived. They've been on their deathbed the minute pain and violation was imposed upon them. The only way to rise from that bed of pain, suffering, and death is to forgive. People can only offer you what they carry within them. People that offer hurt have hurt. People that offer goodness have goodness. People that offer healing carry healing. Continually look at what someone is offering and you'll see clearly what they're carrying. Recognizing what they carry within them helps to either appreciate them more or forgive them quicker."

After the group most of us were talking to each other about what we experienced that day with the apology letters. Every time we shared we healed a little bit more. We not only healed personally but as a group.

The next day in the prevention program we all knew that we were going to continue the discussion from the day before.

After we got settled in Cody announced, "Okay, before we get started I want to tell you something. Not only did what you participate in yesterday take great amounts of courage to write. You all read what you wrote aloud. That's a healthy risk. It's very brave to do such a thing. You're all very good writers with extraordinary vocabularies. All of you are very gifted at expressing yourselves. Healthy communication is the ability to get the pain out and bring the love in. If you use any cuss words in your expression make sure you're using it to accentuate a point, not because you don't have a word to express the feeling. Sometimes cussing is due to a lack of vocabulary, other times it's for emphasis. Here are some dictionaries for each of you to use in the future whenever you're writing. As you build your vocabulary you'll find cuss words aren't even necessary."

I raised my hand and asked the staff if I could share something before we talked more about yesterday's exercise.

Rolo bowed, motioned to the center of the circle and said, "The floor is yours."

"We appreciate and love you guys a lot. Most of us have told you guys you're like family. You're the dads some of us never had. Like the second families and second dads to others. All of the things you teach us, share with us, and use to guide us will never feel as good as if it was our own families and dads doing it. Cody, Dennis, Rolo, even with all the love we feel for you guys we will always wish it was our families and dads who were the ones sharing these things. I just wanted to say that."

Cody empathized, "Thanks for sharing that Carlos. Part of yesterday's exercise was to help with what Carlos shared. We realize we can never take the place of your parents. Our job is not to take the place of your parents. Our job is to give you all the tools you need. We share every bit of information we have with you so you don't need us anymore. Our job is not to make you dependent on us. Our job is to get you to a place where you're interdependent on your skills and other positive influences in your lives. You can never get everything you need from one person, and you should never deny yourself good things that will help you because of one person either. Our job is not to give you more because you were created with everything. Our job is to guide you to get rid of all the pain and hurt that blocks you from all the answers that have *always* been within each one of you."

Dennis exclaimed, "A tribe, community, and a family are groups of people that help each other achieve their optimal potential. They protect each other, honor one another, and love one another. Whatever group does that for you and with you is your family, community, and tribe. Please don't forget the importance of your chosen families and how cautious you need to be when allowing someone into your life. Choose carefully. Great introduction for today, thanks for leading it out Carlos."

Rolo pleaded, "Did you hear what Dennis just said? Let me say it again because it's extremely important. Our job is not to give you more, but to help you get rid of all the things that block you from the love and healing that has *always* been within you."

Cody chuckled as he asked, "What's something that's hard to do in the fog?"

One of the youth answered, "It's hard to see."

"Exactly," Cody said, "and if you're still holding onto hate, resentment and pain then you're in the middle of a fog. The F.O.G. stands for *fear, obligation* and *guilt.* This fog blinds you of your vision and purpose. It misguides you in how you need to think and deal with all the serious things going on in your life. The letters you wrote yesterday are to help you lift the fog from your lives so you don't continue to make decisions based on fear, obligation and guilt."

As usual when Cody spoke with us he gradually moved from calm to passionate and animated.

"Look man. One! The opposite of love isn't hate. The opposite of love is fear. Fear blinds you and makes you think you have to constantly attack or defend things. Two! There's a big difference between your responsibilities and obligations. Responsibilities are things The Creator has placed in your life and in your heart to take care of and make happen. Obligations are things other people impose on you when they want you to be responsible for what they're really responsible for. Three! Guilt is often used by others in an attempt to make you feel bad for the way you *used* to be. Usually none of the *guilty* things others have to tell us about ourselves has anything to do with who we are now and will progress towards in the future. Keep walking the short walk from your head to your hearts. Keep remembering that facing the truth has nothing to do with blame. Get up off the deathbed of hurt-pain-tragedy with the power of forgiveness then you'll see clearer. The fog will gradually lift out of your life and you'll know for yourself that fear, obligation and guilt are useless. They offer nothing that brings us closer to the reason we're born. The fog becomes a great excuse, not a reason, to not look within ourselves. It becomes an even better excuse, not a reason, to keep other people responsible for why we are not living our dreams or walking our path."

Rolo was welling up with tears as he spoke softly and shared something that forever changed the way I viewed so many things.

"It's not about religion. It's about relationships. What kind of a relationship do you have with yourself, creation and The Creator? It doesn't matter if you're Christian, Muslim, Jewish, Buddhist, a traditional person from a Native American tribe, a tribe from other continents, or a Hindu. Regardless of what word you use to refer to The Creator, God, we will all stand before The Creator at some point. We will all answer for the things we did and didn't do."

Rolo paused for a moment then pleaded, "Think about it as if when you're one hundred years old and you pass from this life. You're standing before The Creator. God says, 'I gave you a special talent and ability, why didn't you use it?' You attempt to say that someone else was the reason you didn't use the gifts you were given. God interrupts you and says 'Dear child, they're not standing here with you, it's only us. I didn't give that gift to them. I gave the gift to you. When you were a child you had no choice. You spent your entire teenage years, young adult life, middle age life, and elder life never using the gifts I gave you. My other children who you say were the reason you didn't use your gifts weren't even around you very much after your childhood. The people you blamed never stopped you, *you* stopped you. Every day I hear the cries of my children in every language asking for Heaven on earth. Every day all the gifts I send with each one of my children that can be used to create Heaven on earth aren't being used for that. I listen as so many say in despair and frustration, 'What can I do?' The answer is anything. 'What difference can I make?' The answer is all the difference, even if it's for just one person. 'What's the point?' The answer is that loving Me, your Maker is great, but all the gifts I give are so you children remember how to love one another. You can't truly love Me without seeing Me in all that I created and treating it as Holy.' "

Cody exclaimed, "Wow! I want to be able to tell The Father of creation I used all the gifts and talents I was given to help make Heaven on earth! Good one Rolo!"

"Lots to think about," Dennis said, "Allow me to close this circle with one thing. Consider that the way we see the world and everyone in it is not a fact but a reflection. Blame reflects hurt, forgiveness reflects love. The mirror you use is up to you, but there's always a choice."

Before we got on the agency bus to be taken home after the program that day Dennis, Rolo and Cody pulled me and a couple of other youth aside. They let us know the next day they would be doing a youth violence prevention presentation at one of the high schools. They wanted to know if a couple of my friends in the program and I were up to speaking at the event with them.

I asked, "Why do you want us to speak at it?"

Dennis said, "Well, it wouldn't be much of a youth violence prevention presentation without the voice of the youth would it?"

The other guys and I laughed and said, "True dat."

The next day after school instead of going to the agency, Dennis, Rolo, Cody, a couple other youth and I went to speak at the youth violence presentation. There were some other youth there but mostly adults. After some formal introductions and community announcements Rolo began to present about youth violence prevention within the community.

During part of the presentation one of the parents in the audience stood up and asked Rolo, "Why do kids join gangs?"

Rolo answered, "There's a man by the name of Richard Ramos who has been asking 'Why do most kids *not* join gangs?' I think he's correct because most kids don't and with the *right* questions we can finally get to the *right* answers."

After Rolo said that a bunch of adults started debating with him. A lot of them were saying things like all the kids they see are into something bad and most kids are involved in gangs in our neighborhood. The adults and community leaders were talking amongst one another and it got kind of noisy.

Rolo was laughing and joked with those of us on stage with him. "Well, at least we got the community talking with one other."

I laughed but I knew inside that was another one of those moments where I had to speak. I didn't want to speak but I allowed my heart to push me beyond my fear. I stood up and got the microphone.

"Please hear my words. Do you see me? Because if you do I'm standing here with some other young people who aren't into gangs or anything negative. As a matter of fact we can't get enough of anything positive that's offered to us. I'm not saying my life circumstances are incredibly good or bad. My circumstances aren't any different than anyone else living in our community. Yes, I've seen my share of insanity, death, and violence. I know there are many people who have had way worse experiences than I've had. I'm tired of people comparing tragedies. I want to start comparing miracles in our lives and build on that. I never joined a gang. I'm a regular young person in our community. Adults have to understand even when young people here do all of the *right* things life is still dangerous. Walking the wrong way to school or visiting my friend who has some neighbors that are wyling out; or going to a festival on the wrong day at the wrong time can cost me my life. There are way more good people regardless of age in our community. We just need to step up and keep doing the right things together. Every day I see very few of you out talking with the youth at the spots where we are. Even fewer of you are out on the streets being a healthy competition for gangs, pimps, and drug dealers. You all keep saying the youth are the problem, but you act as if change can happen from behind your desk, from your couch, or from getting together like this once every couple of months to complain about young people. If you're saying the youth are the problem, are you saying you're the solution? If you are the solution, please act like it. We can never have too many good programs and solutions here in our community."

The whole crowd was quiet for about ten seconds until Rolo, Dennis and Cody stood up and started to clap. The audience of adults stood up and joined in the applause. There was some more discussion about what I said. The other youth with us talked about their experiences and thoughts. The whole presentation sparked more ideas and thoughts about solutions instead of blame.

During the ride home from that presentation the youth staff, other youth and I had a good talk. The youth staff let us know they had noticed our speaking ability and vocabulary was developing really nice. They told us they were proud of us for being able to face adversity with a calm and cool demeanor.

I was the last youth they dropped off that night. Before I got out of the van Cody told me, "Carlos, you have to understand the gift of communication you've always had and have chosen to cultivate is *outstanding.* Your vocabulary and ability to deliver your thoughts so people will listen is rare for anyone. When you can effectively communicate there's nothing you cannot do or obtain to make this world a better place. Everything is about communication. It all comes back to your ability to communicate. The better you can communicate the more you can know about yourself and others. You are a young man on a very good road, please *know* this."

I told Cody thank you and before I got out of the van I looked at Dennis, Rolo and Cody and told them, "You'll never know how much you have taught me. I am very grateful for what you've given me. I really appreciate everything, most of all your trust and time."

Dennis yelled, "Enough of the hallmark crap. Get out of the van. I got to get home."

We all laughed and said goodnight.

When I was lying down to go to sleep that night I thought, *one of the reasons why the kids in the neighborhood love the youth staff at the program is because they live in the neighborhood, are from the neighborhood or have worked here so long they might as well be from here. Not to take anything away from the social workers, doctors, teachers and preachers that live an hour or two away. Yeah, they're nice people but that*

only goes so far when you really need someone to relate to what

you're talking about. When there's a lot of details that surround

a situation you can't or don't want to explain, it's easier when

people just know. I can't worry about other people's motives or

intentions. I know who I am and that's just it. I know who I am

now. I like it. It feels good to fall asleep with this kind of peace.

The next day in the program I told Dennis about some of the thoughts I was having before I went to sleep the night before. As usual, he used it as a teaching tool.

"That's an excellent topic for today. Carlos, share some of your thoughts with everyone so we can talk about it."

I explained to the group what I was thinking about the night before. Some of the other youth shared their thoughts and most of us agreed.

I really liked what Rolo contributed to the conversation. "A lot of people give themselves a pat on the back because they got a home run but some of them actually started on third base.

You all are getting home runs and you started at home plate. You all had to go all the way around the bases."

I liked how Rolo said it, because it was cool *and* true.

It was a light day at the program. After a short talk about how far we've come, and how much we've gone through to get where some people start from, we just relaxed.

After the program that day during dinner at my house I told my mom about all the things we covered the past couple of days in the program.

After dinner my mom and I were washing dishes. I felt the need to tell her more about how my perspective about our family has changed. "Mom, there were times I found myself judging our life by things that we have or don't have. I decided what matters most is not what we achieve, but what we've overcome."

"Carlos, you've overcome a lot in a short amount of time. Despite all the obstacles you've had to deal with look at what a magnificent young man you are. I can't tell you enough how proud I am of you."

"And I never get tired of hearing it."

We both laughed.

"Seriously mom, you know I'm past feeling like I'm not good enough or I wasn't the son my dad wanted. I feel good about myself and the vision I have for my future. I feel great about us as a family. I understand what healthy relationships are. I know who my family is. Even though I feel and know all of these things it does hurt that my dad isn't overcoming all these things with us. At times I wonder how far along we would all be if we climbed these mountains together. I forgave him but sometimes I really miss him."

Once again there were tears raining down my face and my head in my mother's arms. It felt good, comfortable, and right. She is the one who taught me stability and consistency.

In the middle of this beautiful moment with my mom and me our front door swung open. I heard a deep voice say, "What's going on?"

I looked over and it was him, my dad was there. We could tell he had been drinking. We were all shocked he was there, but were also happy to see him in a weird kind of way. My mother was just glaring at him. Being a woman of poise she walked into the kitchen to get a glass of water. I knew she was planning something to say but with my mother it was all about timing.

My dad didn't even say hello he just looked at me and started talking. "Why are you crying? Boy you better man up!"

Before I could even answer, my dad asked, "Did somebody beat you up? Because if they did you have to go take your manhood back. Wait, it's a girl right? Cus you know there's a lot more out there, if one doesn't work out it's simple, you just move on. Don't ever let a woman control you. See, this is the kind of thing that happens when you give your heart to someone. Son, you gotta be a man and that means proving your manhood.

Don't sit around and cry that's what little girls do. You aren't a little girl are you?"

My mom was just about to jump in and rip him apart because of his attitude and the way he was talking to me, especially in front of my little brother. I decided to take care of it my way. I thought *I'm the man of the house, right? I'm ready. This is it, the moment of truth, my dad will finally hear me or not, but this is our opportunity.*

I took a deep breath, looked my dad in the eyes and asked, "You're telling me to be a man means I have to go out and prove my manhood?"

"Damn right!"

Although I was pretty sure of what the answer would be I asked, "Why didn't you ever teach me to tie my shoes like you promised?"

"What the hell son you're sixteen years old and still holding on to that? My dad was never there for me neither was my mom. I learned everything on my own. You got it easy but you're sitting here crying about dumb stuff like a little girl!"

I stayed calm because I knew who I was so his drunkenness, anger, and voice didn't intimidate me. I kept pressing him.

"So you learned everything on your own, huh?"

"Damn right I did, nobody gave me anything!"

I could see he was getting aggravated by my questions, but thought, *you come back into our life all of a sudden and you just want us to shut up and listen to your drunken mouth? No, I have some questions and if you don't like it that's your problem.*

"I learned some things on my own too."

"Oh yeah, what's that?"

"While you've been out *proving* your manhood to the world you have two sons here in this home who never questioned your manhood. You never had to *prove* anything to us. It was simple; you're our dad so you're our hero. We just wanted time with you. What I learned is right here."

I handed him a folded piece of paper with something I had written the other day while I was in class thinking about my future and some of my experiences. My dad grabbed the paper and started reading it...

Being a Man

Being a man means my tears cleanse me of hurt so I don't hurt others.

Being a man means I forgive so I don't hurt myself.

Being a man means I'm strong enough not to carry my pain to my children.

Being a man means I know I'm worthy of love and success.

Being a man means I treat women with respect.

Being a man means I learn from my mistakes.

Being a man means I admit when I'm wrong, and then make the necessary corrections.

Being a man means I'm never afraid to apologize.

Being a man means the love I have for my children will be visible in my actions and time.

Being a man means my life will be a testimony of how to live.

Being a man means I'm accountable for my thoughts, actions, and I don't blame others.

Being a man means I'm both gentle and ferocious - a protector and a provider.

Being a man means the evidence of my manhood is in the love and service I give to my family and community.

I was praying the whole time my dad was reading. I was asking The Creator to please allow what I wrote to help my dad begin the short walk from his head to his heart. I watched my dad as he read. His eyes became watery. He began breathing deeper and more relaxed. After he read it he looked at me. I realized I had never seen his eyes like that before. His eyes were soft and it was as if he had one foot up about to take the first step from his head to his heart. Just as quick as that moment was unfolding he pulled it all back inside. His eyes went back to rigid as he withdrew his foot from the path to his heart.

With a great amount of uncertainty he stammered, "I didn't come here for this."

He got up from the chair and slowly walked back out of our house. He didn't walk out the same way he walked in. He moved slower because of the weight of his heart attempting to pull him back to a moment that can't be redone after it's passed. The strength of his anger and pride allowed him to move against the gravity of his heart that was *screaming* for him to do the right thing. It really takes a lot of hurt and a lot of practice to be able to move away from our hearts during moments like those. All the years of exercising his muscles of anger and pride made them strong and instinctual, even with his children. The same muscles that kept him alive and could protect us were the same ones he used to walk away from us.

My dad was like some other men. He was physically strong, quick on his feet and could work all day. He could fight; I never saw it firsthand but heard enough to know he could. He had street smarts and knew how to survive in any situation. The other similarity he had with some other men was that he ran from his kids.

God, Help Me Tie My Shoes

The day after that confrontation with my dad I walked to the program. I didn't go to the program to seek advice, or cry on someone's shoulder. I walked to the program to let the youth staff know they're liars, and I was quitting the program.

I stepped into the youth center. Rolo, Cody, and Dennis were getting everyone together to have a circle. I was hurting bad from the night before. Hurt translates into anger, and I was raging. I felt like I wanted to fight anyone of the youth staff, but Cody was my target.

"Cody, we need to talk, *now*!"

He looked at me inquisitively, and motioned to Rolo and Dennis to handle the group. As he walked towards me he said, "Let's go outside."

We went outside on the lawn of the agency to some picnic tables. Cody sat down but I stayed standing.

"I came here today for one reason. To let you know that you, Rolo, and Dennis are full of crap! Everything you guys taught me set me up for being played. People don't look at me now and see a *man*. People look at me and see *weakness*. Forgiving, living from my heart, speaking with truth, love, and to help; what has it gotten me?!"

"Only you can answer that Carlos."

"It has gotten me *nothing,* except for my dad walking out of my life again. Maybe if I was a *G*, all hard, and living the way I was when I was twelve before I came to this after-school program he would respect me."

"Carlos, I'm not going to try to convince you to do anything you don't want to do. If this is going to be the last day you're here at least tell me what's going on. What happened?"

I told Cody about everything that happened the night before. I exclaimed, "I did everything you guys taught me, *everything.* I confronted him, *yes,* but I did it with love, truth, and to help. I told him and showed him what I learned about manhood. I let him read what I wrote about manhood. I prayed strong. I did it all, Cody. It didn't work, he still left."

I sat down at the picnic table across from Cody. My head was buried in my arms. I felt exhausted. My anger went back to the hurt which caused it, and my tears poured out onto my sleeves.

After a few minutes of letting me cry, Cody spoke sternly.

"Carlos, if you're going to quit, nobody can stop you. If you believe forgiveness and living from your heart has weakened you, I don't know where else to direct you to find *true* strength. However, you are *not* going to leave here today thinking Dennis, Rolo, and I have lied to you."

I interjected, "It didn't work. The things I've been doing didn't keep my dad at our house last night. Those things didn't wake him up. Those things didn't make him proud of me. Those things definitely didn't get him to tie my shoes, or at least explain why he never would. There are no fairytale endings Cody; why are you guys selling us fairytale endings?!"

"The things *you've* been doing have kept you in your house, and in this program. The things *you've* been doing woke you up. The things *you've* been doing made you proud of yourself. The things *you've* been doing have made all the positive difference in the world to your mother, younger brother, and our community."

Cody paused, allowing room for me to speak but I had nothing to say, so he continued.

"We never told you if you give love, truth, and help to others it will be given back to you by *everyone* you share those things with, did we?"

"No."

"What we promised is *even* when others disappoint you; you can look in the mirror and know *you're* a man of love, truth, and help. We never promised anyone a *fairytale* ending. Besides, *fairytale* endings don't just happen, they're chosen; more often than not they're chosen by choosing fairytale *new beginnings*."

"What new beginning? I did everything I believed would get me what I wanted. I prayed and believed God would bless that moment, but my dad still left."

"Carlos, you have unanswered questions like we all do, but there is no such thing as unanswered prayers. The way you described your dad's reaction last night, I know it changed something in him for the better. What are you going to do? Wreck your life, and turn your back on everything until you see the change in your dad? Destroy yourself until you see the prayer answered the way *you* think it should be answered?"

"That's what I feel like doing."

"Yes, it's an option. I've felt the same way about many situations. Like this one time about four years ago a twelve year old kid came into our program. He was hurting bad and we saw it. The more we tried to help, the worse he lashed out at us. No matter what we did he rejected us. I prayed and prayed, thought and thought. I didn't know what else to do because all we offered was love. He didn't know how to receive what he truly wanted, at least not until he knew we wouldn't reject him. He learned we wouldn't give up on him, and no matter how he acted we saw him as a *gift*. Do you remember that kid?"

"I remember him *very* well."

"Maybe it's time you give yourself the gift that forgiveness always offers those who forgive."

"What's that?"

"You already forgave your dad which is very generous. The other side of generosity is being willing to receive."

"Receive what?"

"Your own forgiveness, forgive yourself Carlos."

"For what?"

"Whatever reasons you hold that make you willing to throw your life away because of your dad's choices."

"I didn't do anything."

"Then forgive yourself for thinking you did. You're ready to punish yourself, so you must have blamed yourself."

What Cody said next helped bring me through that moment and many others since that time.

"There are three things to remember for anyone wanting to break the negative cycles within themselves and their family; three things that will have to be used many times and in many situations. The three things are...

Count your scars as the number of times you've been healed, not wounded.

You can't fully develop into what you are, while practicing what you're not.

As long as your life is someone else's fault, it's not your life."

I felt a strong sting of correction when Cody spoke those words, but accepted them because I knew they were with love.

"Carlos, I'm going back inside to help facilitate the group. You can either come inside the agency or walk away; whatever you choose we will always love and respect you. At least give yourself some time out here to think and pray about things before you make the decision."

I said, "Okay." Cody walked back inside the agency and I sat there at the picnic table alone.

I went through all kinds of emotions at that picnic table. I thought *God already forgave me. I already forgave my dad. Maybe it is time to forgive myself. The way I know how to forgive my dad is by keeping my shoes untied, but the only way I know how to forgive myself is by tying them.*

I wrestled with my thoughts and my spirit. I felt if I tied my shoes then I would be giving up a hope I longed for; but if I didn't tie them I would be denying myself the other part of forgiveness. I felt a familiar pain in my chest, just like I had at my first summer camp; but that time as I felt the pain I heard something speak deep inside of me. God's still, small voice in my heart said, *I'll tie them with you, your dad will have other opportunities to make peace with himself. This moment is between us, this moment is for you.*

I yelled, "No!" got up from the picnic table and began walking. The voice became louder within my heart, repeating the same thing over and over. I tried to push the voice out but couldn't. All those years of exercising listening and living from my heart became instinctual, even when I was enraged. I walked around the block and back to that picnic table.

I said, "Okay, You and I will do this together, but will You please heal my dad's broken heart while we tie my shoes?"

I bent over and grabbed the laces. I prayed the whole time as God and I tied my shoes together. When we were done I sat there staring at my tied shoes, reflecting on the decision The Creator and I had made together; a decision that may seem insignificant to some, silly to others, but life changing for me.

While staring at my tied shoes, I realized I had almost made the biggest mistake I could have ever made. In one moment if I would have walked away from my heart's voice I would have began to count my scars as the number of times I was hurt, not healed; I would have possibly spent many years suffering in feeble attempts to embody what I am, while practicing what I am not. I was so close to throwing my dreams away and blaming it on my father. I could have very well spent the rest of my life living by the not-so-uncommon mantras of *they made me this way; he made me this way; she made me this way*. I was dangerously close to my life being someone else's fault, which of course is no life at all.

After much time and reflection at that picnic table I went inside the agency. The group was already over; I had been outside at that picnic table for hours. Cody, Rolo, and Dennis walked up to me. With tear filled eyes each one of them gave me a hug and welcomed me back.

Dennis said, "There have been many young people at the crossroads you were at today who we have never seen again. All the tests you've been through will come full circle for you Carlos and become your testimony; your testimony of *how* to live."

The Sacred Contract of Fatherhood

As a youth I didn't understand what kids did to men like my dad; men who would face death in so many forms, but seeing their own children made them run. The types of men that will run into flying bullets; the men who place their lives and freedom on the line for reputation, pride, and neighborhood. They ran towards the bullets and away from their children. They ran towards a nice car and away from their hearts. They ran towards money and away from their dreams.

As an adult and a father now, I understand what makes some men run from their children. It's easier to run towards things that don't reflect who we truly are; things that don't reveal the best part of us. Those things we search for in so many forms, but run from when they appear because the guilt of the fog tells us we don't deserve it.

My dad didn't have a Rolo, Dennis, or Cody reminding him that he's a gift and Sacred. My dad was used to rejection in many forms. He was never a bad man. He's a man who was beaten down by the voices of lies; lies that he was less than worthy, less than deserving, and less than a miracle. God sent my dad a mirror to remind him of his worthiness; that he is deserving of the best, and most importantly that he is a miracle.

The mirror God sent my dad was his sons. Like some people, when The Creator reminds us of our own beauty, we run. We run to reflections that justify the lies we lived with so long; the lies that begin to intertwine with our own voice; the lies we must sift through to get back to the voice in our hearts.

As the years passed I would see my dad around. We just kept things to small talk. No matter what his reactions were I always made sure I told him I loved him. He was at my high school and college graduations. Now that I'm married to a wonderful wife, and we are blessed with three children, he comes around even more. He has even taught his grandchildren how to tie their shoes. God sent my father another mirror in the form of his grandchildren. This time he is not running from his true reflection, but is embracing it with immense love and gratitude.

It wasn't punishment, guilt, and blame that brought my dad back around. It was forgiveness that made the transition possible. It's forgiveness that allowed my children to know healthy relationships with their grandparents, uncle, mother, and father. Forgiveness broke the negative cycles in my family so my children can grow up with voices ensuring them of their reality...they are gifts, miracles, and worthy of everything good. Forgiveness comes from the one solution to any question asked, Love. Love comes from the source of all life, God.

Many say they believe we're made in the likeness and image of our Creator. I've seen few people act like they believe this when they look at themselves or others. Many people seem to see themselves and others through the very thick fog that blinds us to the reality of the Sacred in all things, including ourselves.

This is another wonderful parent-youth dinner here at the agency. I am honored to have been asked to give my testimony this evening. I am even more honored to give my testimony for the *first* time here at the agency where many healthy changes began to take place within my life. I am grateful to be here. I love seeing many more fathers involved with their children than when I was a participant in this program.

Rolo, Dennis, and Cody, thank you for asking me to give my testimony this evening. Some things take quite a few years to process. It's an honor to work with you guys full-time so I can share my gratitude and healing through the work we do. We're not *better* than the youth we serve; we *are* the youth we serve.

I love learning, and I continue to learn so much from my wife, children, and youth I serve. Even this evening I have just come to understand something, something I have heard Rolo, Dennis, and Cody say for years...my title isn't nearly as important as my testimony.

I'm not going to get into statistics and things like that. You can look those up for yourselves. However, the majorities of young people who are incarcerated, using drugs, involved in gangs, and have run away from home, more often than not have one thing in common...Fathers who are *not* involved in their lives. It is my experience that our highest risk youth are literally killing themselves hoping to achieve their father's attention. At great risk to themselves the youth are calling their fathers back. They long for their fathers to show up, even if it's at their own funeral or to visit them in prison. The extremes the youth are willing to endure clearly shows the importance of fathers. Since youth are fearlessly seeking the light of fatherhood in the dark places of this world; isn't it time for fathers to *fearlessly* deliver the light that will illuminate the darkness for our youth?

What greater gift can a father, stepfather, or healthy male role model give to the children, other than ensuring them they're Sacred and worthy of great blessings? What greater gift can parents give to their children, other than ensuring their children follow the voice within their hearts? What greater gift can fathers who are riddled with guilt give to themselves, other than forgiveness? What greater gift can humanity offer one another to know peace and bring the youth back to the reality of what they are, other than Love? Who better to begin this journey *right now*, other than you?

In closing I would like to explain what for me has become *The Sacred Contract of Fatherhood*.

As fathers we are responsible for guiding the healthy development of our children. The most important aspect of this is nourishing and protecting The Sacred. Every child born is an answered prayer to not only the parents of the child but the world. Every child born brings life-giving water to quench the thirst of dried hearts. Every word and action given to the children in return for the gifts they bring demonstrates how we as fathers see, or don't see ourselves. Every word and action given to the children supports their understanding of what they are, or takes them further from it.

Knowing children as gifts, and Sacred Beings brings forth a healthy and healing strength of humility from within us as fathers. The youth are our teachers with a profound message for the world. When we as fathers acknowledge this Sacredness within ourselves it becomes difficult to *not* acknowledge this within others, especially our children.

To fathers who struggle to see themselves as gifts and Sacred Beings, simply allow your children to remind you of what you've forgotten. At birth, through their new born cries the children sing a song to their fathers and the world. At this very moment hundreds of gifts, Sacred Beings, answered prayers, and messengers of Light are being born in all cultures and languages. They're all entering this world singing *The Sacred Contract of Fatherhood...*

You cannot be entrusted with something you're not.
It's alright if you've forgot.
I'm here to remind you so that we remember together.
And bring others with us on the most important endeavor –
On Earth as it is in Heaven

About the Author

Anthony Goulet began working with high-risk youth in the field of prevention and intervention in 1991. He has led gang prevention and intervention programs as well as prisoner reentry programs. He has worked as a Certified Addictions Counselor with gang affiliated youth and adults providing relapse prevention for substance abuse and criminal behavior. Anthony is contracted by organizations to facilitate trainings on gang prevention, gang intervention, conflict resolution and cultural competency. Anthony currently resides in Dallas, Texas with his wife and children where he works full-time as a gang interventionist.

To purchase the book and for other inquiries please visit:

www.realwarriorslove.com

About the Forward

Joseph Brave-Heart was born on the Pine Ridge Reservation in 1968, and was removed just prior to the "Reign of Terror" in the 1970's which was the culmination of 100 years of abuse, neglect, and unrealistic political policies. It was in this time that much of the so-called "old ways" and elders were lost. Dr. Brave-Heart has studied and implemented the teachings of the people for the past 24 years, in ceremony and daily life. The preservation of language, cultural protocols, stories, ceremonies and ethics as a cultural philosophy has been his primary goal for the benefit of the generations to come. As a sun dancer his pledge is for the children and future generations. Joseph received his doctorate in Divinity in 2009.

To Contact Joseph Brave-Heart send an email to:

braveheartjoseph@yahoo.com

About the Cover Artist

Michael Kelty's work is about exploring the human experience. He finds people to be the most interesting element in our world. Michael looks into and weighs the conscious and subconscious, the external and internal, the depth of the human spirit and life's experiences and how we are shaped by what we say and do. When he creates a work of art, he implements emotion and character which produces an extension of that person or experience. His art is a compassionate ritual that expresses the mysterious nature of the human spirit.

To contact Michael Kelty for designs, paintings, creative consultation or other inquiries please visit his website at:

http://michaelkelty.com

Made in the USA
Charleston, SC
13 September 2012